NUMBER THIRTY:

*The Walter Prescott Webb
Memorial Lectures*

The African Diaspora

THE AFRICAN Diaspora

by
Joseph E. Harris
Alusine Jalloh
Joseph E. Inikori
Colin A. Palmer
Douglas B. Chambers
Dale T. Graden

Edited by Alusine Jalloh
and Stephen E. Maizlish

Published for the University of Texas
at Arlington by
TEXAS A&M UNIVERSITY PRESS
College Station

The paper used in this book meets the minimum
requirements of the American National Standard
for Permanence of Paper for Printed
Library Materials, Z39.48-1984. Binding materials
have been chosen for durability.
∞

Library of Congress Cataloging-in-Publication Data

The African diaspora / by Joseph E. Harris . . .
    [et al.]; edited by Alusine Jalloh and Stephen E.
    Maizlish. — 1st ed.
        p.   cm. — (The Walter Prescott Webb
    memorial lectures ; no. 30)
    Includes bibliographical references.
    ISBN 0-89096-720-2 (cloth, alk. paper)
    ISBN 0-89096-731-8 (paper, alk. paper)
    1. African diaspora.   I. Harris, Joseph E.,
    1929–   . II. Jalloh, Alusine, 1963–   .
III. Maizlish, Stephen E., 1945–   .   IV. Series:
Walter Prescott Webb memorial lectures; 30.
DT16.5.A325   1996
960 — dc20   96-20906
                                                          CIP

Contents

Preface

This book is the result of the thirtieth in the series of annual Walter Prescott Webb Memorial Lectures, "Africa and the African Diaspora," held on March 9, 1995, at the University of Texas at Arlington (UTA). Contributors to this volume include nationally recognized scholars on Africa and the Africa diaspora. Alusine Jalloh, author of the introduction, is an assistant professor of history and a founding director of the Africa Program at the University of Texas at Arlington. He studied history at the University of Sierra Leone and obtained his Ph.D. at Howard University. With David E. Skinner, he is currently coediting *Islam and Trade in Sierra Leone,* and he authored two chapters of this forthcoming publication. In addition, he is completing a book-length study of Muslim Fula merchants in post-colonial Sierra Leone. His research interests include African entrepreneurship in West Africa.

Joseph E. Harris is distinguished professor of history at Howard University. He has authored three books: *African-American Reactions to War in Ethiopia, 1936–1941* (1994), *Repatriates and Refugees in a Colonial Society: The Case of Kenya* (1987), and *The African Presence in Asia: Consequences of the East African Slave Trade* (1971). He is editor of *Global Dimensions of the African Diaspora* (1993) and three other works. In addition, he has served as a consultant to UNESCO and the United States Information Agency.

Colin A. Palmer is distinguished professor of history at the City University of New York. He had contributed many articles to American and Latin American journals and is the author of four books: *The First Passage: Africans in the Americas, 1502–1617* (1994), *Passageways: An Interpretive History of Black America* (1994), *Human Cargoes: The British Slave Trade to Spanish America, 1700–1739* (1981), and *Slaves of the White God: Blacks in Mexico, 1570–1650* (1976). With Franklin Knight, he coedited *The Modern Caribbean* (1989).

Joseph E. Inikori is associate director of the Frederick Douglas Institute for African and African-American Studies and is professor of history at the University of Rochester. In addition to his numerous scholarly articles, he is the author of *The Chaining of a Continent: Export Demand for Captives and the History of Africa South of the Sahara, 1450–1870* (1992) and *Slavery and the Rise of Capitalism: The 1993 Elsa Goveia Memorial Lecture* (1993). With Stanley L. Engerman, he coedited *The Atlantic Slave Trade: Effects on Economies, Societies, and Peoples in Africa* (1992), and he edited *Forced Migration: The Impact of the Export Slave Trade on African Societies* (1982). Professor Inikori has also served as a consultant to UNESCO.

Dale T. Graden, cowinner of the Webb lectures essay competition, is assistant professor of history and director of the Latin American Studies Program at the University of Idaho. His research interests focus on comparative slavery and emancipation in the Atlantic World. His article "'An Act . . . Even of Public Security': Slave Resistance, Social Tensions, and the End of the International Slave Trade to Brazil, 1835–1856" is forthcoming in the *Hispanic American Historical Review*.

Douglas B. Chambers, the other cowinner of the essay competition, is a Ph.D. candidate in history at the University of Virginia. He is writing his dissertation, "The World They Made Apart: Africans, African-Virginians, and the Development of a Slave Culture," under the supervision of Joseph C. Miller.

Stephen E. Maizlish is associate professor of history at the University of Texas at Arlington. A specialist on the Civil War in the United States, he is the author of *The Triumph of Sectionalism: The Transformation of Ohio Politics, 1844–1856* (1983). He has coedited three books: *New Perspectives on Race and Slavery in America* with Robert Abzug (1986), *Walter Prescott Webb and the Teaching of History* with Dennis Reinhartz (1985), and *Essays on American Antebellum Politics, 1840–1860* with John Kushma (1982).

On behalf of the UTA History Department, the editors would like to acknowledge several benefactors of the Webb lectures. C. B. Smith, Sr., an Austin businessman and former student of Walter Prescott Webb, generously established the Webb Endowment Fund and made possible the publication of the lectures. Jenkins and Virginia Garrett of Fort Worth have long shown both loyalty and generosity to UTA. Recently the Webb lecture series has received major support from the Rudolf Hermann's Endowment for the Liberal Arts. Dr. Wendell Nedderman, former president of UTA, was instrumental in obtaining this funding and has always been a steadfast supporter of the lecture series. We would also like to acknowledge the assistance of Kenneth R. Philp, chairman of the history department, and the dedication of Steven G. Reinhardt, chairman of the Webb Lectures Committee at UTA.

Alusine Jalloh
Stephen E. Maizlish

The African Diaspora

Introduction

ALUSINE JALLOH

          In the last three decades scholars from various disciplines, especially history and anthropology, have conducted detailed research about the African diaspora in Asia, the Americas, and Europe, as well as trading diasporas of Africans on the vast and diverse African continent.[1] These diaspora-oriented studies have expanded our understanding of the presence and contributions of people of African descent outside the continent. They have also expanded our appreciation of the internal movement of Africans and the subsequent creation of ethnic minority communities on the continent itself.

    The African diaspora was born out of the voluntary and involuntary movement of Africans to various areas of the world since ancient times, but involuntary migration through the trans-Saharan, trans-Atlantic, and Indian Ocean slave trades accounts for most of the black presence outside of Africa today. The concept of the African diaspora has also come to include the psychological and physical return of people of African descent to their homeland, Africa. Today, the historical relationship between Africans and their descendants abroad is a major subject not only in history but in other disciplines as well.

    Trading diasporas in Africa, on the other hand, resulted from the mostly voluntary migration of Africans to communities where they form ethnic minorities. This phenomenon dates back several centuries and occurred in many areas of the continent. Most of the current inter-disciplinary research has focused on ethnic minority communities in West Africa. Often, the African migrant communities were involved in chain migration from their homelands to their host countries, but they maintained various social ties with their homelands. Moreover, mi-grants also established extensive kinship networks that extended into their homelands. These kinship networks were an important aspect of the organizational structure of the internal and cross-boundary trading of ethnic migrant groups in Africa.[2]

Despite the availability of good studies on trading diasporas in Af-rica, more research is needed to explore the internal and cross-boundary mercantile activities of ethnic groups with a long history of migration on the continent, such as the Fulas.[3] There is also a need for additional studies that will explore the social and political relationships between immigrant communities and host societies. Moreover, the geographic focus of trading diaspora studies should be broadened to cover ethnic minority communities outside of West Africa, especially in southern and eastern Africa. Much has already been written on the Yoruba and Hausa trading diasporas in West Africa.

The collection of essays in this volume represent important contri-butions to the scholarship on the African diaspora and trading diasporas in Africa; topics include African business history, African slavery, and the experience of African slaves and their descendants in the diaspora. They are written from different perspectives by historians of African and non-African descent and build on the multi-racial scholarly collaborative tradition that now accounts for the vast body of knowledge on the Afri-can past and that of people of African descent abroad.

Joseph E. Harris's essay, which presents an overview of the African diaspora, is a fitting backdrop to this collection of articles. Not only does he affirm the black diaspora as an extension of the African heritage, he also discusses the origins and dispersal of Africans through voluntary and involuntary migrations since ancient times. In addition to distin-guishing historical and modern black diasporas, he shows how the Afri-can diaspora affects the economies, politics, and social dynamics of both the homeland and the host country or area. This historical relationship between Africans and their descendants abroad remains an important subject in diaspora studies. Harris concludes that diasporas are signifi-cant factors in national and international relations.

The chapter by Alusine Jalloh reconstructs the history of the Fula trading diaspora in colonial Sierra Leone, part of a larger diaspora in West Africa. In discussing Fula merchant capital, he focuses on the variety of mercantile activities, sources of capital, management practices, types of investments, and the role of Islam and kinship networks in Fula entrepreneurship. Moreover, he examines the relationship between Fula immigrant merchants and the host society. By focusing on Muslim Fulas, who have played a major role in shaping the religious and commercial landscapes of Sierra Leone over the past two centuries, this study complements a number of good general studies on trade and Islam in Sierra Leone.

African slavery, which is central to an understanding of the origins of the African diaspora, is the subject of Joseph. E. Inikori's essay. In an attempt to define and clarify the institution of slavery in Africa, as well as set it in a world context, Inikori undertakes a comparative study of servile social categories in medieval Europe and pre-colonial Africa. He argues that slavery and serfdom under the socio-economic conditions of medieval Europe provide better comparative insights for a study of pre-colonial Africa than the New World comparisons that have been documented by scholars to date. This analysis is carried out against the backdrop of the definitional shifts in the historiography of slavery in Africa.

The next three essays deal with various aspects of the black experience in the Americas. Colin A. Palmer revisits American slavery by focusing on the various aspects of the lives of slaves. In interpreting American slavery from the perspective of the enslaved people of African descent, he contends that we cannot fully grasp the meaning of slavery for the enslaved unless we have a deeper understanding of the power relationships that shaped the institution and the variety of ways in which African slaves were mistreated in the Americas. His essay argues for the inclusion of the experiences and internal markers of people of African descent in the reconstruction of their history. Moreover, it stresses the importance of an understanding of African culture in explaining the lives of the enslaved, whether from the perspective of the impact of slavery or the resistance of the enslaved.

Douglas B. Chambers's essay explores African slave culture in eighteenth-century Virginia. Chambers traces the historiographical shifts since the Herskovits-Frazier debate and documents the enduring influence of Africanisms—those elements of culture found in the New World that are traceable to an African origin—in the historical development of Afro-Virginian slave culture. Drawing on the lives of the enslaved in eighteenth-century Virginia, Chambers shows the African influences on the historical culture they created in their creole world. His essay builds on a number of good interdisciplinary studies that attempt to reconstruct the cultural survivals of African slaves and their role in the creation of the multi-dimensional culture of African Americans in the United States.[4]

The volume concludes with Dale T. Graden's examination of African slavery in Salvador, Bahia, in Brazil between 1848 and 1856. In focusing on the crisis faced by the Bahian elite — which resulted from slave resistance, the outbreak of a yellow fever epidemic, and the appearance of formal abolitionist expression in Salvador — Graden argues that the crisis ended only after the abolition of the international slave trade to Brazil in 1850, the reexport of slaves out of Bahia as part of an internal slave trade, and the outbreak of a cholera epidemic in 1855–56 that devastated the population of Salvador and Bahia. The institution of slavery remained an integral part of the regional economy until slave resistance and a resurgent abolitionist movement led to an emancipation decree in 1888.

The collection of essays in this volume demonstrates the range of possibilities for innovative scholarship on various aspects of the global African presence and ethnic trading minorities in Africa. I hope that it will inform readers and stimulate further research on the African diaspora and trading diasporas in Africa.

NOTES

1. See, for example, Joseph E. Harris, ed., *Global Dimensions of the African Diaspora* (Washington, D.C.: Howard University Press, 1993); A. J. G. Wyse, *The Krio of Sierra Leone* (London: Hurst, 1989); W. A. Shack and E. P. Skinner, eds., *Strangers in African Societies* (Berkeley: University of California Press, 1979); and A. Cohen, *Custom and Politics in Urban Africa: A Study of Hausa Migrants in Yoruba Towns* (London: Routledge and Kegal Paul, 1969).

2. See Philip D. Curtin, *Cross-Cultural Trade in World History* (Cambridge: Cambridge University Press, 1992), pp. 1–59.

3. The Fulas are also known as Fulbe, Peul, Fulani, or Fulatta in West Africa.

4. See, for example, Joseph E. Holloway, ed., *Africanisms in American Culture* (Bloomington: Indiana University Press, 1990).

The Dynamics of the Global African Diaspora

JOSEPH E. HARRIS

The African diaspora is a triadic relationship linking a dispersed group of people to the homeland, Africa, and to their host or adopted countries. Diasporas develop and reinforce images and ideas about themselves and their original homelands, as well as affect the economies, politics, and social dynamics of both the homeland and the host country or area. Diasporas are therefore significant factors in national and international relations.

In recent years the term *diaspora* has become increasingly common in studies of African, Chinese, Indian, and other communities outside their original homelands. These communities reside in and have loyalty to their adopted country but also identify with and maintain connections to their country of origin. This relationship helps explain the depth of complexity in the dynamics between the people in these communities, their homelands, and their host countries. Thus, it is important that we understand the historical development and impact of the linkages between Africa and its diaspora communities.

Historically, the Jews and Irish have received considerable attention as diaspora communities with influence abroad. However, the study of diasporas is especially timely today because of the current fragmentation and displacement of people throughout the world: in Eastern Europe, for example, the former Yugoslavia and the Soviet Union; South and Southeast Asia, especially India, Vietnam, and Cambodia; and Africa, notably Ethiopia, Somalia, and Rwanda. More recent and urgent for Americans is the mass immigration of Haitians, Cubans, Mexicans, Vietnamese, and Chinese into the United States. These diaspora groups share characteristics of ethnic identity, marginality, and homeland linkage, and one can not understand them without an examination of their original homelands and the root causes and specific contexts within which they were dispersed.

The case of Africans and their descendants abroad is especially complex, with a long history of international dispersion, stereotypes, and myths that continue to obstruct policies and practices to guarantee freedom and justice.[1] The facts in this instance are fairly well-known and are rooted in centuries of Africans being characterized as inferior, destined to be slaves, incapable of developing complex societies, lacking a meaningful cultural history, and uncivilized and thus having made no contribution to world civilization; this list could be expanded. These myths and variations of them persist in spite of evidence to the contrary. Yet recent research amply demonstrates the dynamic and rich heritage of Africa and its diaspora: abundant evidence of African achievements in continuing archaeological discoveries; the reconstruction of ancient and complex societies in Africa and their impact on other parts of the world; the commercial relations of Africans, Arabs, and Asians in the Indian Ocean since ancient times; the creative art of Benin, Dogon, and other African societies; the literary accomplishments of Africans in pre- and early Islamic Arabia; the roles Africans played in the rise and expansion of Islam and Christianity; the early relations between Mali, Kongo, and other African states with Portugal prior to the slave trade; and the many accomplishments of Africans and their descendants in Europe and the Americas.

This essay, then, will examine the global dispersion of African peoples since ancient times, making a distinction between the historical and modern diasporas, will provide evidence of the continuity of their consciousness of and identity with Africa, and will assess the gradual transformation from African to African American and the implications of that development. Although primary focus on the African diaspora has been placed on the slave trade, one should remember that Africans traveled voluntarily throughout much of the world long before the slave trade existed. In ancient times they traveled as merchants and sailors, many of whom settled in Europe, the Middle East, and Asia. Some came as soldiers and remained permanently. There are many examples of Africans engaged in sports and the arts in the Middle East and Europe, and some of these people became residents. Others served as missionaries for Islam and Christianity and settled in the Middle East, Asia, and Europe. Several Ethiopian monks accompanied European Crusaders to Rome, Florence, Venice, Portugal, and Spain, and a number of Ethiopian royal emissaries traveled to and remained in Europe, especially Rome, in the Middle Ages. Free Africans also participated in the exploration and development of the Americas: Canada, the Caribbean and Central America, and North and South America. Long before the Age of European Exploration, Africans, like other people, traveled abroad as free persons and often settled in their host countries.

It was, however, the slave trade that made the African presence essentially global. For at least fifteen hundred years prior to the European-conducted trade in African slaves, Arabs conducted a slave trade across the Sahara Desert, the Mediterranean Sea, the Red Sea, and the Indian Ocean, and they took Africans to Arabia, India, and the Far East. Enslaved Africans worked in the Persian Gulf in salt mines, coconut groves, and date plantations; in Bahrain as pearl divers; in India as palace guards; in Arabia and India as domestics and field hands; and throughout much of the Muslim world as concubines and eunuchs.

Today discrete communities of African descent can be found in Iran (Bander Abbas, Jiruft, Shiraz, and Tehran), in Iraq (Baghdad and Basra), in Pakistan (Karachi, Lahore, and Baluchistan), and in India (Hyderabad, Ahmadabad, Surat, Cutch, and Gujarat). Many people of African origin reside in communities of mixed descent throughout Asia. Little evidence has appeared to identify contemporary African descendants in China and Japan dating from this period, although the historical record shows that Africans were taken to Macao, Hwangchou, and Nagasaki in the sixteenth century.

The largest number of enslaved Africans were settled in India. Known as Siddis and Habshis, Africans served as administrators, guards, sailors, and farm hands. Large numbers of enslaved and free Africans served in Muslim armies in Gujarat in the thirteenth century, and in India today there remains the Habshi Kot, an Ethiopian fort with tombs of African soldiers and nobles.[2] During the Medieval period Europeans and Arabs captured and sold Africans in the Mediterranean area. Africans were shipped from Tunis and Cyrenaica to Barcelona, Genoa, Naples, Turkey, and the Middle East. Indeed, Africans were settled along wide stretches of the northern Mediterranean coast.

It was the European Age of Exploration in the fifteenth century, however, that led to the greatest dispersion of Africans in history. Although occurring in a shorter time-frame than that of the Arabs, the European-conducted slave trade enveloped the continent. In 1444 a company was established in Lagos, Portugal, to engage in the slave trade. That year some 240 bonded Africans were appropriated by Prince Henry, the church of Lagos, the Franciscans of Saint Cape Vincent, and some merchants. By 1448 a regular trade in goods and Africans had been established between Arguim and Portugal. Africans worked in the mines, at construction, on farms, and as guards, soldiers, domestics, couriers, stevedores, concubines, and factory workers. Slave communities were established in Lisbon, Barcelona, Cadiz, Seville, and Valencia. Africans were also taken to the Spanish possession of The Netherlands.

In spite of the fact that Queen Elizabeth I in 1556 observed that there were too many "blackamoores" in England and that they should be returned to Africa, their numbers continued to grow, so that by the nineteenth century there were some fifteen thousand in England. Slavery also emerged in France, despite a royal proclamation prohibiting it. Both enslaved and free Africans lived in the cities of Anjou, Lyon, Orleans, Nantes, Marseilles, Toulon, and Paris, where they worked as servants, menial laborers, pages, and entertainers.[3]

Other parts of Europe also became home for Africans, both enslaved and free. Some joined the small communities of Ethiopian monks in Venice, Rome, and neighboring cities along the northern Mediterranean rim; others settled along the southern Adriatic coast of what today is Yugoslavia. The city of Ulcinj in particular had a number of Africans who in the sixteenth and seventeenth centuries worked as seamen in the straits of Otranto. Of eastern Europe we know very little, except for the great-grandfather of Aleksandr Pushkin, who was reexported from Turkey to Russia.

When the Europeans defeated the Arabs and took control of the Indian ocean trade routes, they developed their own slave trade from Zanzibar and other regions of Africa's eastern coast to Asia. Europeans also took Africans from what today are Kenya, Tanzania, Mozambique, and Madagascar along the southern route, around the Cape of Good Hope to Buenos Aires in Argentina, Montevideo in Uruguay, and Rio de Janeiro in Brazil. Africans were marched overland from Buenos Aires and Montevideo through the passes of the Andean Mountains to enslavement in Santiago and Valparaiso in Chile; from Rio de Janeiro through Paraguay and Bolivia to Lima and Callao in Peru.

The northern route from East Africa extended around the cape to northern Brazil and into the Caribbean, where some Africans were sold and others were transported to North American cities such as Mobile, Charleston, and Richmond. Cartegena in Colombia became a major port from which enslaved Africans were taken overland to the Pacific coast of Choco. Others were transported to and across Panama to the Pacific coasts of Ecuador, Peru, and Chile.

The well-known Guinea coast of West Africa was the area from which European slave dealers took most of the Africans enslaved in Europe and the Americas. As early as the 1440s Africans were taken from Arguim to Portugal and sold. Enslaved Africans became more common in Spain, France, and England during the sixteenth century. Gradually the Portuguese developed tropical plantations on the offshore African islands of Cape Verde, Sao Tome, and Principe, thereby establishing a relationship between the plantation economy and enslaved African labor, both of which they transferred to the Americas.

The other major area of intensive slave trading was around the mouth of the Congo River in Zaire and upper Angola, which supplied large numbers of captive Africans to Brazil and the Caribbean Islands, as well as North America. Again, most of the Africans who reached North America were transported via the Caribbean, where they were first "seasoned."

Although not part of the slave trade, the convict labor system used by the British to populate a number of their colonial possessions constituted another means of African dispersion abroad. Convict labor drew from the prison population, which included debtors, thieves, and other criminals. The Africans in this group were usually vagrants who could not find employment in a racially biased society. At least several hundred of the original Australian settlers were Africans.

There is no way to know the exact number of Africans who were transported and enslaved abroad, but the best estimates are those for the Americas: a total of between 12 and 25 million Africans reached the American hemisphere; many others perished during the trans-Atlantic voyage. Of the arrivals, most went to Brazil, followed by the British Caribbean, the French Caribbean, Spanish American areas, and North America.[4]

Despite the inhumane nature of the capture and enslavement of Africans, cultural continuities persisted for years in multiple ways throughout the diaspora. Africans who arrived abroad continued to speak and practice their native languages and traditions, especially during the early years and in the privacy of their quarters, homes, and social groups: they sang and danced as their cultures had taught them, referred to themselves as Africans and Ethiopians, and gave their children African names. Neither the Middle Passage nor the slave system broke their awareness of their history. This is revealed in their religious practices (Candomblé and Santeria especially), songs, and oral traditions. Their culture and aspirations for freedom were expressed in different forms (songs, poetry, religion) and were sometimes employed to solidify mass followings in resistance movements, such as the ninth-century revolt in Iraq, in which Rihan Ibn Salib established an autonomous community that replicated African traditions; the sixteenth century revolt in Mexico, in which Yanga sought to replicate Guinea; the seventeenth-century revolt led by Zumbi in Brazil, in which Palmares adopted African traditions and remained autonomous for most of that century; the eighteenth-century revolt in Haiti initiated by the African-born Boukman and the Christian, diaspora-born Toussaint L'Ouverture, and which resulted in independence; and the abortive nineteenth-century revolt in Virginia, led by the African Gullah Jack and diaspora-born Nat Turner. All of these freedom movements incorporated traditional symbols and ceremonies around which Africans rallied.[5]

As important as was the struggle for freedom, it must be emphasized that Africans did much more than think about their enslavement. They were primarily occupied with daily life, which necessitated creativity and a degree of accommodation to local conditions. These Africans were concerned about family and community life, with such social organizations as churches, lodges, and mutual aid and burial groups. They learned European languages and culture; in time some converted to Christianity. In Asia they learned Arabic, Farsi, Gujurati, Urdu, and other languages, and some of them converted to Islam. Throughout Europe and Asia they distinguished themselves as artists, writers, poets, teachers, and inventors. This gradual transformation from African to African American or African European, for example, helps to explain the complexity and dialectical contradictions in the relations between the African diaspora and the homeland, the phenomenon behind W. E. B. DuBois's concept of "double consciousness."[6]

This necessarily brief discussion of the historical diaspora confirms a global dispersion and settlement of Africans, who settled abroad voluntarily and involuntarily and maintained a consciousness of their homeland and their identity while adapting to new societies. This phase of the diaspora was largely a heritage of the slave trade and enslavement, but it was also a period of abolitionism and the establishment of colonial rule in Africa itself during the nineteenth century. The convergence of these two phenomena resulted in the globalization of black economic and political dependence on Europeans with the consequent global entrenchment of the age-old negative images, myths, and stereotypes about Africans and their descendants.

The abolition of the slave trade reinforced African hopes to return to their homeland and increased efforts by Europeans and Americans to return them to Africa. Efforts by the former were poorly financed, encountered many obstacles, and in fact only drew from the small free community; efforts by the latter were more successful and encouraged a number of slave owners to free Africans with the stipulation that they return to Africa. Slave ships were intercepted and captive Africans were freed and initially settled at selected points outside of Africa: Florida, briefly, for the Atlantic trade, and India, Aden, and the Seychelles for the Indian Ocean trade.

These temporary stations were replaced by permanent resettlement efforts as missionary and business groups in England and the United States realized that diaspora Africans could serve as a means to rid Europe and America of unwanted blacks and at the same time establish communities that could both expand the Christian faith and commerce and also be regarded as humanitarian. Thus it was that Sierra Leone in 1787 and Liberia in 1821 became permanent resettlement communities in West Africa for ex-slaves from the Atlantic Ocean countries, and Freretown in Kenya became the resettlement point in 1873 for ex-slaves from the Indian Ocean areas. While some African descendants abroad opposed "return to Africa" movements, others saw these projects as a means to achieve freedom, launch the redemption of the African continent, and establish themselves as viable members of the world community.[7]

When Sierra Leone and Kenya became British colonies, the diaspora sentiment was muted, although not destroyed; Liberia, however, declared its independence in 1847 and became the second independent African country, after Ethiopia, until well into the twentieth century. By 1867 some twenty thousand African Americans had settled in Liberia and many of them had been free in the United States and returned voluntarily with material resources. Liberia thus became a symbol of hope for the regeneration of Africans on the continent and in the diaspora. Its Declaration of Independence took note of the plight of African peoples abroad and committed the country to "provide a home for the dispersed children of Africa." Although these returnees carried with them ideas of superiority taught in the United States, they did identify with Africa, which they hoped to redeem and lead into the modern world.

This return movement from the United States coincided with a growing consciousness of and identification with Africa by African Americans. A number of their church and social groups had already adopted "African" as a label and engaged in activities in the Caribbean and Africa. Indeed, although they were influenced by white denominations, black churches provided the principal opportunities for the development of sustained and meaningful links with Africa and the diaspora and the outside world.

Thus a common social condition and origin, stemming largely from the centuries-old slave trade and slavery, became more deeply embedded in the black consciousness of the diaspora. Europeans and Americans regarded enslaved Africans as chattel and free blacks as inferior beings. One of the best illustrations of this situation occurs in the American Declaration of Independence and the Constitution, in which both the concepts of freedom and inhumanity are embedded. The former portrays European settlers as victims who escaped political and economic inhumanity in Europe and who established a refuge for liberty in the American colonies, while the Constitution defines Africans as three-fifths of a white person. Other provisions of that document allowed "fugitive" (African) slaves to be tracked down like animals and treated as property. Subsequently, in 1858 the Supreme Court declared that blacks had no rights that whites had to respect.

While amendments to the Constitution have declared citizenship rights for former slaves, there never has been a constitutional recognition of the horrendous European and Euro-American inhumanity to Africans in Africa and their descendants abroad, nor has there been a strong, sustained effort by the government or the people as a whole to establish and protect African American humanity since liberation — abolition and civil rights movements notwithstanding. Stereotypes and myths about black physical and mental incapacity persist and continue to obstruct equity and justice for African Americans as a group.

A determining factor in the relations between Africans in Africa and their descendants abroad stemmed from decisions made by Europeans at the Berlin Conference of 1884–85, which essentially established the boundaries of the African states.[8] This partition of Africa divided peoples and cultures into different countries, making them "citizens" by fiat. It initiated a new phase of population displacement and division, created an internal diaspora, and led to irredentist movements that plague the continent today.

The colonial-era partition and dispersion of Africans was marked by an accelerated gravitation of Africans to and settlement in major cities of the colonial powers: France for the Senegalese, Malians, Ivoriens, Haitians, Martinicans, Guadeloupeans, and others from French-speaking areas; England for the Ghanaians, Nigerians, Kenyans, South Africans, Jamaicans, Trinidadians, Barbadians, and others in English-speaking areas; Portugal for the Angolans, Mozambicans, Cape Verdians, and Brazilians; the Netherlands for the Surinamese; Belgium for the Zairians; and the United States during the late colonial period and especially after World War II. The major cities of the Western powers thus became loci for the gathering of diverse ethnic and political groups of African origin, facilitating the development of an international network linking Africa to its diaspora; this network may be called a mobilized diaspora.

The critical factor about the earlier, primarily involuntary diaspora is that it occurred prior to the partition of Africa and therefore had no consciousness of the boundaries established during the era of colonial rule. Although the dispersion during the colonial era did begin to internalize a consciousness of the colonial territory, most Africans did not directly or fully confront the colonial presence. When the colonial era ended, after less than a century in most cases, the colonial identity had not fully matured. Consequently, until the 1960s most Africans in Africa retained a primary ethnic allegiance, while their descendants abroad constituted a "stateless" diaspora without a common country of origin, language, religion, or culture. The strength of the connection between Africans and the African diaspora remained essentially their common origin in Africa as a whole and a common social condition (social, economic, and political marginalization) throughout the world.

It was this combination that paved the way for the development of an effective international network by the mobilized African diaspora, namely, descendant Africans with a consciousness of the identity of their roots, occupational and communication skills, social and economic status, and access to decision-making bodies in their host country. For blacks this meant the mobilization of their communities around race or ethnicity for the exertion of political pressure on elected officials. In time they elected members of their own group to offices at virtually all levels of local, state, and national government.

From the early years of the twentieth century, African American migration from southern states resulted in the gradual emergence of large segregated communities in such northern American cities as Washington, Philadelphia, New York, Detroit, and Chicago. This pattern of migrations increased significantly after World War I. In these cities African Americans found better educational and employment opportunities, which also attracted black immigrants from Caribbean countries, notably Jamaica, Barbados, Trinidad, and Panama. New York City was the principal recipient of this emerging international community of blacks.

A somewhat similar development was occurring in England, where London's black community was expanding with immigrants primarily from Jamaica, Barbados, and Trinidad. London had long been a place where blacks from the West Indies, the United States, and Africa were familiar as abolitionists, businessmen, journalists, scholars, and travelers. As early as 1900 Henry Sylvester Williams of Trinidad and W. E. B. DuBois of the United States had convened the first Pan-African Congress to mobilize African people in a coordinated international effort against racism in the African colonies and communities of blacks in the diaspora.[9]

Although the congress demonstrated that Africans and their descendants abroad shared common interests and were prepared to seek a common means to satisfy their concerns, it was not until after World War I that the Pan-African movement would have a sustained impact. DuBois revived the movement and convened four congresses (in 1919, 1921, 1923, and 1927) with similar objectives of human rights for African peoples.

Marcus Garvey, a Jamaican, arrived in the United States in 1916 after having travelled widely in the Caribbean and South America, where he protested against white exploitation of blacks. In the United States he organized the Universal Negro Improvement Association (UNIA), with branches throughout much of the African world. His newspaper, *The Negro World,* appeared in English, French, and Spanish and made a strong appeal for black unity, pride, and organization. His Black Star Line was organized not only to transport blacks who wanted to go to Africa but also to initiate commercial relations between Africa and its diaspora. Although his projects failed and he was deported from the United States, Garvey contributed immeasurably to the development of a consciousness of Africa in the diaspora and to racial pride and organization. Garveyites continued his tradition by maintaining branches of UNIA and participating in numerous organizations dedicated to black progress.

DuBois and Garvey were giants of their time, but there were many others who contributed significantly to the cause of Africa and its diaspora between the two World Wars: Casely Hayford and Kwame Nkrumah of Ghana, Ladipo Solanke and Nnamdi Azikiwe of Nigeria, Duse Mohammed of Sudan, Jomo Kenyatta of Kenya, Candace Gratien of Guadeloupe, Leopold Sedar Senghor of Senegal, Leon Damas of Guyana, Aimee Cesaire of Martinique, Jean Price-Mars and Dantes Bellegarde of Haiti, Ras Makonnen of Guyana, and George Padmore and C. L. R. James of Trinidad.

A number of less well-known but important leaders and organizations either joined the better-known groups or organized their own to mobilize African peoples worldwide: William Leo Hansberry and William R. Steen organized the Ethiopian Research Council in the United States: Malaku Bayen, an Ethiopian, organized the Ethiopian World Federation in the United States; Max Yergen, W. E. B. DuBois, and Paul Robeson organized the International Committee on Africa, which became the Council for African Affairs; C. L. R. James organized the International Friends of Ethiopia in London, with branches in the United States and the Caribbean; George Padmore, a Jamaican, and Ras Makonnen, a Guyanan, organized the International African Service Bureau in London; and Alioune Diop, a Senegalese, organized the Society for African Culture in France, while John A. Davis and others organized an affiliate in the United States, the American Society for African Culture. In short, members of the mobilized diaspora pioneered the establishment of international organizations promoting African consciousness and solidarity in what essentially became a foreign relations movement. Prevented from being actors in state foreign affairs, these leaders established their own non-state mechanisms for the conduct of foreign affairs in the interests of Africans and their descendants abroad.

The Congressional Black Caucus in 1960 represented a major step toward the official participation of blacks in the foreign affairs of its country. Mobilized black voters elected three congressmen who became the founding members of the Caucus. The membership increased to forty in 1992 and gave the organization significant political influence. Caucus leaders soon realized that their impact on foreign policy centered on African world issues, and, without conceding their right to input on foreign affairs generally, they embraced Africa and the Caribbean as their special domain. Members of their staffs followed by forming the African Forum on Foreign Affairs, which soon evolved into TransAfrica, the established lobby for African and Caribbean issues in the United States. Its influence on U.S. policy regarding South Africa and Haiti in particular has legitimized it as a force in world politics for Africa and its diaspora.

The dynamics of black nationalism in the African world during the last generation has transformed the meaning of identity in Africa and the diaspora. Whereas the diaspora of the slave trade era was essentially "stateless," relying primarily on an Africa remembered, the post-independence diaspora promotes a consciousness of new nations, sometimes with new names and ideologies that challenge the older diaspora to make choices between conflicting interests not only within the diaspora community, but also between it and particular African countries. The existence of over fifty African countries with varying social and political conditions and different international interests further complicates the relationship between Africa and its diaspora. Moreover, the legacy of colonial internal division and dispersion of ethnic groups form a kind of diaspora that African states must confront also.

In the United States, diverse interests and ideologies are evident, and they are complicated by the continuous influx of continental Africans and Americans of African descent from the Caribbean and increasingly from South American countries. Consequently, the geographical area of focus for African Americans has been expanded to include French-, Spanish-, and Portuguese-speaking areas of the Americas.

Noteworthy in this modern phase of the diaspora is that whereas prior to independence continental Africans and African Americans used non-governmental networks (churches, social groups, schools, etcetera) as the principal conduit for the promotion of their ideas and policies, independent African leaders must negotiate their interests through governments and their representatives, thereby excluding effective non-governmental agencies of the diaspora. While this approach maximizes economic dimensions for African states, it minimizes the cultural and social dimensions that continue to sustain the mutual identity between them and their diaspora, a significant political force in time of need.

If direct and effective relations are to be cultivated, Africa and its diaspora must devise other structures to achieve their goals. This could take the form of a non-political organization or foundation that reaches across national boundaries and that represents African governments and private organizations and diaspora groups for broad consultative purposes and humanitarian assistance. The African world would benefit greatly from having this kind of international structure with the financial capability to initiate and fund programs without reliance on outside financial or political support. Such autonomy would enable Africans and their descendants abroad to sustain their political presence and work with greater confidence in alliance with other groups interested in their social, political, and economic well-being.

Such a form of Pan-Africanism is better described as TransAfricanism, best demonstrated in the 1930s when Ethiopia resisted Italian aggression. Organized groups of Americans of African descent in the United States mobilized efforts and contributed money, supplies, and advisers to assist the Ethiopians during and after the war. These groups also ventured into private diplomacy: developing a code, communicating directly through their network with Haile Sellassie, and persuading him to appoint a representative to the United States. These efforts demonstrated the strength the diaspora could display when compelled to action by African issues. In addition, the reciprocal involvement of Ethiopians with these groups heightened the political consciousness of African Americans and contributed to their greater participation in the democratic process of their country.

A particular problem that has prevented the fuller development of this trend has been the diversity of the groups involved and the scope of issues African Americans have attempted to address internally while pursuing issues under the rubric of Pan-Africanism or TransAfricanism. The independence of over fifty African countries and a dozen in the Caribbean continue to divert attention and limited material resources.

The last decade of the twentieth century is marked by countries and cultures being pulled closer together by technology, world health issues, and international trade. Moreover, the United States has emerged as the lone superpower and is thus obliged to respond to issues of world significance. As the preeminent country of mobilized diasporas, the United States can enhance its role by enlisting its diasporas as bridges to troubled lands — as teachers, scientists, technicians, and emissaries for peace and development.

Over the centuries African Americans, by their sustained struggle for justice, have contributed significantly to the positive international image of this country's potential for real democracy. They have remained in the vanguard of struggles for human rights for minorities, women, and other under-represented groups. From the abolitionist travels and egalitarian appeals of Frederick Douglass and others in the nineteenth century to Martin Luther King and Malcolm X in the twentieth and to the adoption by Africans, Asians, and Europeans in freedom struggles of the anthem "We Shall Overcome," African Americans have aligned the United States with struggles against racism and colonialism. It is no accident that two of the five black Nobel Peace Laureates — Ralph Bunche and Martin Luther King — are African Americans; the other three — Albert Luthuli, Bishop Tutu and Nelson Mandela — are South Africans, whose heritage in many ways parallels that of African Americans.

Blacks in the United States are conscious of their relationship to the global African presence; they have a long and steadfast tradition of association not only with African people, but also with other minorities, with the poor and disadvantaged, and with women. African Americans have remained in the vanguard of the struggle for human rights and since the 1930s have increasingly asserted themselves in international affairs. The twenty-first century may well witness the convergence of this heritage and the skills of the diaspora with the political and economic development of Africa and thus the full participation of the African world in international affairs.

NOTES

1. St. Clair Drake, *Black Folk Here and There,* 2 volumes (Los Angeles: Center for Afro-American Studies, 1986, 1990) is a major source for a study of the global presence of African peoples; Joseph E. Harris, ed., *Global Dimensions of the African Diaspora* (Washington, D.C.: Howard University Press, 1993) includes essays on various regions, concepts, and themes relevant to the African diaspora.

2. Bernard Lewis, *Race and Slavery in the Middle East* (New York: Oxford University Press, 1990); Joseph E. Harris, *The African Presence in Asia: Consequences of the East African Slave Trade* (Evanston, Ill.: Northwestern University Press, 1971); Harris, "Scope or the African Diaspora" (Silver Spring, Md.: African Diaspora Maps, 1990).

3. See *The African Slave Trade from the Fifteenth to the Nineteenth Century* (Paris: UNESCO, 1979); Ibrahim B. Kake, *Les Noires de la Diaspora* (Libreville, Gabon, 1978); Leslie Rout, *The African Experience in Spanish America* (Cambridge: Cambridge University Press, 1976); Folarin Shyllon, *Black People in Britain* (London: Oxford University Press, 1977).

4. Philip D. Curtin, *The Atlantic Slave Trade: A Census* (Madison: University of Wisconsin Press, 1969), although dated, remains a valuable source; Joseph Inikori, *Forced Migration* (New York: Africana 1982) is an excellent study that revises much of Curtin's work.

5. For cultural manifestations in the Americas, see Robert Farris Thompson, *Flash of the Spirit* (New York: Vintage, 1984). For revolts, see Alexandre Popovic, *La Révolte des Esclaves en Iraq au IIIe/IXe Siècle* (Paris: P. Geuthner, 1976); Colin Palmer, *Slaves of the White God: Blacks in Mexico, 1570–1650* (Cambridge: Cambridge University Press, 1976); Manuel Carneiro da Cunha, *Negros, Estrangeiros* (São Paulo, Brazil: Brasiliense, 1985); C. L. James, *Black Jacobins* (New York: Vintage, 1963); Frederico Brito Figueroa, *Venezuela Colonial: Las Rebelliones De Esclavos Y La Revolucion Francesa* (Caracas, Venezuela: CIHALC, 1989); and Harris, *Global Dimensions of the African Diaspora.*

6. W. E. B. DuBois, *Souls of Black Folk* (New York: Fawcett, 1961).

7. Arthur T. Porter, *Creoledom: A Study of the Development of the Freetown Society* (London: Oxford University Press, 1963); Akintole Wyse, *The Krio of Sierra Leone: An Interpretive History* (Washington, D.C.: How-

ard University Press, 1991); Tom Shick, *Behold the Promised Land: A History of Afro-American Settler Society in Nineteenth Century Liberia* (Baltimore: Johns Hopkins University Press, 1980); Harris, *Repatriates and Refugees in a Colonial Society: The Case of Kenya* (Washington, D.C.: Howard University Press, 1987).

8. A. I. Asiwaju, *Partitioned Africans: Ethnic Relations Across Africa's International Boundaries, 1884–1994* (Lagos: Lagos University Press, 1985)

9. See Vincent Thompson, *Africa and Unity* (New York: Humanities Press, 1969); W. E. B. DuBois, *The World and Africa* (New York: 1947); J. Ayodele Langley; *Pan-Africanism and Nationalism in West Africa, 1900–1945* (Oxford: Clarendon Press, 1973); Ras Makonnen, *Pan-Africanism From Within* (New York: Oxford University Press, 1973); and Drake, "Diaspora Studies and Pan-Africanism," in Harris, ed., *Global Dimensions of the African Diaspora,* pp. 451–514.

The Fula Trading Diaspora in Colonial Sierra Leone

ALUSINE JALLOH

For over two hundred years prior to the independence of Sierra Leone in 1961, Fula merchants contributed to the country's development, as is documented in several historical studies.[1] While such works are useful in providing us with a broad picture of Fula commerce, they fail to provide sufficient details about the variety of Fula trading activities, types of investments, and business management. This paper will examine these aspects of Fula commerce in colonial Sierra Leone and will demonstrate that Fula merchant capital was not dependent on foreign capital, that Fula merchants did not benefit from state patronage, that Islam constrained long-term Fula capital growth, and that Fula immigrant psychology inhibited long-term capital accumulation.

The role of Fula merchant capital is situated within the framework of the British colonial economy in Sierra Leone. This economy comprised a market and subsistence sector connected in a relationship in which the market economy prevailed. Despite marked differences between the two sectors, they had a common backbone: agriculture. In contrast to African domination of the subsistence sector, Europeans exercised greater influence in the market economy. During the colonial period the Sierra Leonean economy underwent modifications of varying degrees that were largely brought about by external events.

Clearly, the Sierra Leonean economy was dependent on the British economy and was structured to realize primarily the raison d'etre of British colonialism: the monopolistic exploitation of Sierra Leone. The main purpose of having colonies in West Africa was to secure a profitable trade for the colonizing country. Until 1945, the economic policy of the British colonial administration was primarily laissez-faire and aimed at financial self-sufficiency for Sierra Leone. According to British policy, Africans should bear the greater cost of administering the colony. Therefore, the colonial administration instituted a system of taxation to raise revenue. Colonial investment was limited and restricted to sectors of the economy that directly served British interests, such as the railway. The European trading companies operated with minimum regulation in consonance with the official policy of free trade. The collection of custom duties on imports and exports was perhaps the single most important economic role of the colonial administration.

The post–World War II era witnessed a new British policy of direct participation in the economies of her colonies. To finance the improvement and expansion of such sectors of the Sierra Leonean economy as agriculture, the colonial administration utilized money appropriated by the Colonial Development and Welfare Acts in Britain. These changes facilitated British exploitation, which lasted until the colony's independence.[2]

In sum, the colonial economy in Sierra Leone, as in colonies elsewhere, served metropolitan interests. Indeed, merchant capital was a cornerstone of this economy, as evidenced by the colonial emphasis on trade. But African merchants, including Fulas, occupied a secondary position in the country's commercial hierarchy, which was dominated by Europeans.[3]

MERCHANT POPULATION

The Fula merchants in colonial Sierra Leone were part of a broader diaspora in West Africa. Several studies have been done on the Fulas elsewhere in West Africa detailing their pastoral mode of existence, mercantile pursuits, and Islamic activities.[4] In Sierra Leone they were mostly immigrants from Fuuta Jalon in Guinea and Senegal. As a Muslim immigrant population, the Fulas maintained a high level of cultural exclusiveness with few cross-ethnic marriages in the multiethnic environment of Sierra Leone. This may be explained by the strong Fula adherence to Islam and the assumed Fula cultural superiority over the rest of the Sierra Leone population.

Many of the Fula immigrants settled in Freetown, the capital city, where they undertook mercantile activities. For these Fulas, the good life was the combination of commercial success and the progressive attainment of Islamic learning, and they saw Freetown as a place where these goals could be realized. Sierra Leone's utilities and industrial, commercial, financial, and educational institutions were concentrated in the capital. Therefore, the city became the focus of urban migration and the most densely populated area of the country.[5]

The Fulas in Freetown were part of a larger diaspora in Sierra Leone which included the Koinadugu District, where the Fula diaspora is concentrated, today Tonkolili District, Bombali District, Kailahun District, and Pujehun District in the Sierra Leone Protectorate.[6] Fula migration to these areas dates back to the seventeenth century, but the major waves of migration occurred in the eighteenth and nineteenth centuries. Like the Fulas who migrated to Freetown, these Fulas were motivated by commercial reasons. They also played a major role in the spread of Islam in the Sierra Leone hinterland through the establishment of educational institutions and proselytizing. Although nomadic and itinerant, many of these Fula migrants became sedentary and created Islamic communities among the indigenous inhabitants. Moreover, some families such as the Bundukas in the Northern Province and the Kai Kais in the Southern Province even created political ruling classes in their communities. Some of these Fulas accumulated capital through trading before resettling in Freetown to take advantage of greater economic opportunities. They traded in various merchandise, including kola, cattle, and palm oil, within the Protectorate and between this area and Freetown. Many of them maintained their trade networks with the Protectorate after they settled permanently in Freetown.[7]

Within the male-dominated Fula immigrant community there was a patron-client relationship grounded in kinship ties between settled, wealthy Fula *julaabe* (merchants) and newly arrived, poor Fulas in Sierra Leone. As patrons, the *julaabe* provided their kinsmen clients with free food and free lodging, obtained valid immigration documents for them, and gave them an opportunity to acquire commercial skills as assistants in their various trading undertakings. Eventually, they would provide their clients with capital to launch their own *julaagol* (trading careers). The clients would reciprocate with unremunerative labor and commercial, political, and social loyalty.

Interpersonal relations among the Fula merchants were based on loyalty and trust grounded in Islam. These factors shaped not only the merchants' commercial relations, but their entire social interaction and were also evident in their relations with non-Fula immigrant traders, such as the Mandinkas. It was in the area of credit that trust based on Islamic faith was very important among Fula merchants, as well as in their commercial transactions with Muslim traders from other ethnic groups.

In contrast to many ethnic groups, the Fula merchants did not have voluntary associations that integrated them into the Sierra Leone social fabric. Instead, they had *jokereendhan* (social solidarity), a cultural practice that brought together Fulas, irrespective of social class, to help one another in diverse ways. This practice was demonstrated in both difficult times and in celebrations.

In the context of commerce, *jokereendhan* motivated many wealthy Fula merchants to give interest-free loans, as well as non-repayable start-up capital, to allow poor, newly arrived Fula immigrants to undertake trading. In contrast to some mercantile groups such as the Temne, the Fula immigrants did not have credit mechanisms such as the *esusu* (rotating credit associations). Place of origin was of great importance in Fula inter-personal relations, notwithstanding *jokereendhan*. A new migrant expected more help from Fulas from his own settlement of origin than from others. There was also more trust between Fulas coming from the same place. New immigrants tend to do business with landlords from their settlement or origin. Similarly, business landlords tend to recruit clients from their home settlements when possible.[8]

As immigrants, the Fula merchants experienced marginality in colonial Sierra Leone, resulting primarily from their lack of Western education, which was then heavily influenced by Christianity. Although Western education was the single most important factor for integration into the host society, the vast majority of Fula merchants did not manifest any inclination to acquire even its rudiments because they believed it would compromise their Islamic faith.[9]

The Fula mercantile community was linked with the wider multi-ethnic Muslim trading population in Sierra Leone, and Islam was an important factor integrating these merchants. Fula immigrant traders had limited commercial and social networks outside the Muslim mercantile community. Their lack of Western education and their Islamic faith inhibited the establishment of well-developed commercial relations with non-Muslim merchants.[10]

As a merchant class the Fulas were well-organized, frugal, shrewd, low-key, had considerable self-confidence, and enjoyed taking on new problems and identifying solutions. They could make decisions and stick to them. Also, they were practical and had reasonable expectations about what they and their employees could accomplish. Overall, they had a long-range vision of what could be accomplished, both in the short term and long term.

COMMERCIAL ACTIVITIES

In colonial Sierra Leone, the major commercial activities of the Fulas were the cattle trade and its related butchering business, the retailing of merchandise, and the diamond business. These mercantile occupations were not mutually exclusive. Rather, Fulas pursued diverse trading careers in their search for profits. Diversification was very common among the Fula merchants, especially those in the urban areas, because they wanted to spread business risks, increase profits, and provide employment to kinsmen.

CATTLE TRADE

Of all Fula commercial activities in colonial Sierra Leone, the earliest was the cattle trade. Since the seventeenth century itinerant Fula *julas* (cattle traders) had brought cattle from Fuuta Jalon to Sierra Leone, especially to Freetown. This trade was important to the British colonial administration because Sierra Leone depended on Fuuta Jalon for cattle supplies, as is revealed in a secret memorandum from 1945, in which the Governor stated that "the cattle trade is essential to the maintenance of meat supplies in Sierra Leone."[11] The colonial administration was committed to maintaining a low-cost meat supply for the rapidly growing Freetown population, and this required that the Fula-dominated cattle trade with Fuuta Jalon be sustained.

Because Fuuta Jalon was the largest source of cattle supply, the colonial administration continuously frustrated French efforts to control the cattle trade and to prevent the smuggling of cattle across the boundary.[12] The French colonial authorities made several complaints to the British Governor in Sierra Leone over this issue, but the British continued to oppose French attempts to regulate the cattle trade. A secret memorandum of November 8, 1943, by the British Chief Secretary of State, West African Council, to the Secretary of State for the Colonies in London stated that "Sierra Leone strongly oppose [sic] proposal to bring cattle trade under French control."[13]

Some of the cattle sold by the Fulas in Sierra Leone came from the Koinadugu District and the Bombali District, where the Fulas had begun permanent settlements. These Districts are close to Fuuta Jalon and share a similar climate and vegetation. In addition, they have the largest area of savanna-type vegetation in the country. The climate in these northern areas is also less humid than the south.[14]

Fula-owned *nagge* (cattle) were of the N'dama type, which have no hump, in contrast to the large Zebu cattle kept by Fulas in Senegal, Mali, Burkina Faso, and Northern Nigeria. N'dama cattle are also resistant to the deadly disease trypanosomiasis, spread by the tsetse fly. They are small, about four hundred pounds when fully grown. Finally, they are raised primarily for meat; they do not produce much milk.

A key role of the Fulas in the cattle trade was that of *julas*. They came from different areas of Fuuta Jalon and northern Sierra Leone to sell their cattle in various markets, especially the Freetown market. The *julas* arrived alone as well as in groups. Often, butchers provided them with free lodging and food until they returned to their homelands.

In Freetown, while some *julas* brought their cattle directly to butchers, others went through the Soso, who served as landlords and brokers in the coastal town of Bullom in northwestern Sierra Leone. In return for introducing the *julas* to butchers, ensuring fair prices, and providing food and lodging, the Bullom brokers received a negotiable commission from the *julas*. The *julas* were often paid between two and four weeks after reaching an oral price agreement with the Freetown butchers.[15]

Besides the Bullom landlords, there were Fula cattle brokers, such as *Moodi* (title of respect in Pulaar) Tija Jalloh-Jamburia and *Alhaji*[16] Abdulai Jalloh, who made *ous moni* ("house money," or commissions) selling cattle to cross-ethnic Freetown butchers. Like their Bullom landlords, they provided food and lodging to the *julas*. As cattle brokers, these Fulas received *ous moni* of as much as twenty shillings on every cow sold to a butcher. In some instances, they would buy cattle directly from the *julas* and sell them to Freetown butchers.

In addition to their role as *julas,* the Fulas also functioned as *jorkal* (cattle middle-men), whose responsibility was to travel to different parts of Fuuta Jalon to purchase cattle for the Sierra Leone market. This was an especially vital service when there was a shortage of cattle in the country. The employers of *jorkal* were mostly wealthy Fula butchers, such as the legendary *Alhaji* Momodu Allie, who migrated from Senegal to Sierra Leone in 1904. The cultural and religious affinity between the butchers and *jorkal* translated into low labor cost and dependability, two crucial factors for success in this sector of trade.

As in the cattle trade, the Fulas dominated the related multi-ethnic butchering business, which included Mandinka, Krio, Temne, Soso, and

Lebanese butchers. The butchering business involved the supply of meat to the public and to institutions such as hospitals and the military. There was intense intra-ethnic and cross-ethnic competition among the butchers to secure the meat-supply contract with the colonial administration and to sell meat to the multi-ethnic public, but ethnic solidarity also existed. The Muslim Fula butchers, for example, exploited their ethnic and religious affinity with Muslim Fula *julas* to succeed over butchers from other ethnic groups.

Alhaji Allie was the wealthiest Fula butcher in colonial Sierra Leone. Between 1908 and 1948 he made over £200,000 in profits by supplying meat to the public and the colonial administration. In Freetown the public market for meat was largely dominated by Krio professionals, who purchased meat mostly on Tuesdays and Saturdays. Christmas was the peak season because Krios purchased large quantities of meat to celebrate their holiday. The Lebanese were also an important group of consumers; they bought meat mostly on Saturdays. Muslim consumers purchased large quantities of meat mostly on the Muslim holidays: *id-ul-fitr* (marking the end of Ramadan), *id-ul-adha* (commemoration of Abraham's sacrifice), and *maulid-ul-nabi* (celebration of Prophet Muhammad's birthday). Meat was affordable at a retail price ranging from eight to ten pence per pound.

Most of *Alhaji* Allie's meat sales to the colonial administration went as rations to indigenous and British troops stationed in Sierra Leone during World War I and World War II; local soldiers served under a British officer in the Sierra Leone Battalion of the Royal West African Frontier Force (R.W.A.F.F.). During World War II the colonial administration also provided meat as rations to *manawa* (British war ships) in transit in Freetown en route to the South Atlantic. Because of its natural harbor and mountain ranges, Freetown was of great strategic importance to the British Navy and Air Force in the war in the South Atlantic. It is estimated that over ten thousand British troops were stationed in Freetown between 1939 and 1945.[17]

Fula management of the cattle trade and butchering business was characterized by the centralization of decision-making by the owner. This management style stemmed largely from the belief that commercial details should be kept private within the family or kinship group. Such centralization was a common feature of all Fula mercantile activities in colonial Sierra Leone.[18]

Besides business centralization, kinship played a major role in the management of Fula mercantile activities. The Fulas preferred kinsmen to work in their businesses; thus, there was a high degree of consanguineous and affinal kinship among members of the Fula merchant class. Individual merchants sought to solidify their social and business positions through the use of the kinship system. Consanguineous and affinal ties produced groups of merchants who, if not in actual partnership, were loyal to each other and interested in each other's prosperity. It was not uncommon for a powerful merchant to have sons, sons-in-law, brothers, brothers-in-law, nephews, cousins, and grandsons tied to each other not only by blood and marriage, but by an ever-expanding net of commercial interests. Important merchants such as *Alhaji* Allie strengthened their social and business positions by creating such kinship groups.[19]

MERCHANDISE TRADING

The retailing of provisions such as bread and bottled mineral water in shops was a major aspect of Fula private enterprise in colonial Sierra Leone. Between 1900 and 1961 the number of Fula-owned shops in Sierra Leone grew from fifty to over three thousand. The Fula shopkeepers, popularly known as *kotoos* (a title of respect in Pulaar), were retailers who bought provisions from European, Lebanese, and Indian wholesalers to sell to consumers. Although the Fulas were at the end of the commercial distribution of provisions in the colonial economy, they provided a convenient and important service to consumers. The vast majority of the Fula shopkeepers were concentrated in residential urban areas, and their customers were drawn from the immediate neighborhood. This proximity to consumers enabled Fula shopkeepers to make quick profits. Most of them used their homes as shops as a cost-saving practice, facilitating the accumulation of more trading capital.[20]

Many of the Fula shopkeepers during the colonial period were immigrants who derived their capital from menial labor, working as domestic servants, "shop boys," or "watchmen" (night security). Their employers were mostly Krio professionals and Lebanese and Indian merchants. These occupations were disdained by most urban residents. Some of the Fula shopkeepers were former self-employed *worok* (porters) in the major markets of Freetown, such as King Jimmy at Water Street. According to several Fula shopkeepers, they suffered indignities for years in their endeavor to save trading capital from their wages from their menial jobs. It was also during such periods of menial employment that some Fulas developed trust with Lebanese and Indian merchants, who would later provide merchandise on credit.

Fula shopkeepers were predominantly male. In Fula cultural practice it was the responsibility of *Fulamusube* (Fula women) to bear children and take care of the home. The *Fulamusube* and indigenous wives of these shopkeepers ran the business only when their husbands made periodic visits to their homelands in Guinea or Senegal; such visits often lasted from one to three months. If the Fula shopkeeper had two or more wives, he would assign responsibility for running the shop to the *beyngu aranoh* (first wife), while the others rotated the household responsibilities. Children who had acquired some Western education usually helped with balancing the books and obtaining supplies. When the husband returned to Sierra Leone, the *beyngu aranoh* would provide a comprehensive account of how the business and household were run in his absence.

The trading enterprises of the Fula shopkeepers involved both nuclear and extended family members. The owner of the business, usually the father, made all the management decisions, while other family members played supporting roles. Some wealthy Fula shopkeepers opened shops for each of their two, three, or four wives at different locations in urban areas. Kinship networks were important in the commercial organization of Fula shopkeepers in terms of credit allocation and business expansion. Wealthy Fula traders provided their kinsmen with *nyamande* (credit) in cash or goods to open their own businesses. In keeping with their shared Islamic faith, the recipients repaid these loans without *riba* (interest) at their convenience. Well-established Fula merchants also provided interest-free loans and monetary gifts to kinsmen to expand their trading enterprises.[21]

Kinship affinity also brought together Fula shopkeepers in business partnerships to procure merchandise wholesale from Lebanese, European, and Indian merchants. The goods were divided according to the size of the capital invested by each partner and then retailed to consumers. In so doing, the merchants overcame the problem of small individual capital; they also gained the upper hand over competitors trading in similar goods bought at relatively expensive retail prices.

The Great Depression of 1929 changed the commercial landscape of the Fulas in Sierra Leone. Many who had started as hawkers became urban shopkeepers in the aftermath of the Great Depression. This situation was paralleled by the decline of Krio shopkeepers, who were dependent on European firms that suffered from the economic hardship and decline induced by the Great Depression. European companies such as the United Africa Company (UAC) undertook extensive reorganization of their commercial networks. They closed many branches and amalgamated others and systematically withdrew from retail merchandising or trade. These activities created opportunities for entry into retail trading, which the Fulas exploited. The Fula merchants were marginally affected by the Great Depression because, unlike the Krio merchants, they were not dependent on European trade credit.[22]

As business owners, the Fulas were responsible for supervising their employees and planning the direction of and promoting their businesses. These responsibilities were critical. By employing kinspeople, Fula merchants made their business operations cost-effective and time-efficient. Since they shared the same culture, it took Fula business owners less time to train kinsmen to run their operations.

In addition, as self-employed merchants, Fula shopkeepers had three advantages. First, owning their own businesses offered a potentially greater income stream than was generally available to an employee. There was usually a correlation between hard work and economic return. Second, being self-employed offered the Fulas greater independence and stability than working for others, such as the Krios. Third, because they were in control of their own time and were free to spend it as they saw fit, the Fulas could engage in many satisfying activities, such as Islamic proselytizing, that were not available to employees.[23]

THE DIAMOND BUSINESS

From the mid–1950s to the end of the colonial period in 1961 the Fulas increasingly became involved in the diamond trade of Sierra Leone. Since the early 1930s, when diamonds were first discovered there, Kono, in the Eastern Province, had been the center of diamond mining in colonial Sierra Leone. The Consolidated African Selection Trust (CAST) was the first company to prospect and to discover large amounts of diamonds in the area. Its subsidiary, the Sierra Leone Selection Trust (SLST), was then formed to mine the diamonds. In 1934 the colonial administration gave the SLST exclusive rights to mine diamonds in Sierra Leone for ninety-nine years in return for certain payments to the colonial administration. In 1952 a new agreement made the SLST subject to new income tax laws operating in Sierra Leone.[24]

Because of widespread smuggling, the colonial administration decided in 1956 to restrict the mining activities of the SLST and to grant licenses to individuals to mine diamonds in Kono. This program, the Alluvial Diamond Mining Scheme, brought about a diamond boom that attracted several ethnic groups, including Fulas, in Sierra Leone and elsewhere in West Africa. One such Fula was *Alhaji* Mohammed Bailor Barrie, who migrated to Kono from Kabala in northern Sierra Leone and later became a legendary businessman in post-colonial Sierra Leone. The vast majority of Fulas in the trade were engaged in illicit alluvial diamond mining in the towns of Yengema and Sefadu in Kono.[25]

The Fulas developed extensive kinship networks in the diamond trade. Some of them provided money to their kinsmen to mine diamonds on the understanding that if diamonds were found they could purchase them below the market price. To expand their trade contacts with the indigenous diamond traders and miners, the Fulas developed fluency in several Sierra Leonean languages. They also entered into business partnerships with Kono political leaders and the owners of some of the mining sites.

Besides working with Sierra Leonean diamond traders and miners in Kono, the Fulas also developed a close working relationship with Muslim immigrant diamond traders such as the Mandinkas and Marakas. Shared Islamic faith was a major factor in bringing these merchants together. Most of the immigrant diamond traders came from Guinea, Senegal, Mali, and the Gambia. They were attracted to Kono by the prospect of quick profits from diamond sales. They were often told by wealthy returning kinsmen about the great opportunities that Kono offered to those who were willing to take risks in the diamond business.

Because of their limited knowledge of the market outside of Sierra Leone and their desire to make quick profits, the Fulas sold most of their diamonds to Lebanese middlemen for substantial profits. By 1961 the Lebanese had established themselves as major buyers of illicit alluvial diamonds from Fulas and other immigrant diamond traders in Kono. Some Lebanese actually owned mines, where they employed Sierra Leoneans and immigrants such as Fulas.[26]

Hard evidence on the volume and value of diamond sales by Fulas in the colonial period is difficult to obtain because of the illicit nature of the business and the participants' reluctance to divulge personal financial information. Because Fula merchants generally believed that their diamonds would be confiscated and that they would be imprisoned because they did not have valid immigration documents and mining licenses, they did not report sales to the Government Diamond Office (GDO), the only legitimate exporter of diamonds in Sierra Leone. In fact, the Sierra Leone Government announced that after January 29, 1959, illicit diamond diggers would face a penalty of twelve months imprisonment. Despite Fula circumvention of the GDO, we do know that they sold over £500,000 worth of diamonds prior to independence.[27]

Profits from the diamond trade were ploughed back by the Fulas into various sectors of the Sierra Leonean economy, such as transportation, retail merchandise, and the cattle trade. They saw the diamond trade as the fastest way to generate sufficient capital to diversify into various businesses, but considered it to be a risky enterprise that did not warrant long-term investment of capital. They saw other areas of the economy, such as real estate, as safer investments for their profits.

INVESTMENTS

In colonial Sierra Leone, the bulk of the Fula merchants' investments was in urban and rural properties, seen as secure and not subject to the risks of bad loans or oversupply, problems besetting commercial trade. Besides, real property was mortgageable and could thus be used to expand credit. It could also easily be transferred to one's heirs. Fula properties included houses, small apartments and rooms for rent, small shops rented to merchants, and vacant lots. Property investments ranged from £5 to more than £2,000.

Alhaji Allie possessed the largest urban property in absolute value in colonial Sierra Leone. He owned more than ninety properties worth over £100,000 in Freetown when he died in 1948. They were concentrated in the Central Business District of the city, which included Kissy Street, Kissy Road, Rawdon Street, and Little East Street. These properties were rented to indigenous business owners, West African immigrants, and Lebanese traders, who were mostly retailers of imported merchandise.

The vast majority of the Fula merchants obtained their properties through cash purchases from the profits of their businesses. In Freetown many of the sellers were Krio families who had long owned most of the real estate in the city. For several decades before Fula merchants entered the real estate sector of the Freetown economy, Krios had used their commercial profits and professional income to purchase urban properties that passed from one generation to another.[28]

Besides properties, *jawdi* (livestock) were also an important Fula long-term investment. The exact number of Fula-owned cattle during the colonial period is not known because of poor record keeping; private records suggest they numbered over two hundred thousand. Historically, Fulas used cattle as an item of trade, as well as a store of wealth, throughout West Africa. In colonial Sierra Leone, Fula merchants in various trading occupations invested in cattle kept in *warehs* (cattle ranches). *Alhaji* Allie, for example, had eighteen *warehs* in different areas of Freetown, such as Calabar Town and Hastings. At the height of his butchering career during World War II, *Alhaji* Allie had as many as eight hundred cows in one *wareh* alone.[29]

To Fulas, cattle were also used as both convertible and short-term investments. Some Fula traders sold their cattle for cash to finance new mercantile pursuits for themselves or their children. This was how *Alhaji* Bailor Barrie entered the diamond business in Kono.[30] They also used profits from the sale of cattle to pay for *hajj* (pilgrimage) expenses for themselves and their relatives, as well as to finance the education of their children in Islam abroad. The number of cattle sold in this manner was very small. For Fula cattle owners, it was inconceivable to be without cattle; therefore, they sold as little as possible.[31]

Despite their major investments in real estate and livestock, Fula merchants did not realize their full investment potential in colonial Sierra Leone. From the Great Depression to the end of the colonial era, they had many opportunities to take over failing Krio and European businesses, to expand from retailing merchandise to wholesale trade, and to increase their real estate holdings by buying low-priced properties, but this not happen for two reasons. First, the vast majority of the Fula traders who had substantial capital were immigrants who saw such business expansion as a long-term commitment that required them to stay longer than they wanted in Sierra Leone. These Fula traders came to the area only to buy clothes and salt for themselves and their relatives in their homelands. Despite this attitude, a few wealthy merchants such as *Alhaji* Allie repeatedly encouraged their fellow Fula traders to invest in properties, even if their stay in Sierra Leone was temporary. Paradoxically, the evidence shows that most of these immigrants either died in Sierra Leone or remained there into the post-colonial period. Second, Fula merchants were unwilling to borrow investment capital from foreign-controlled banks because of their religious objection to interest payment. Because of the Fulas' well-earned reputation as dependable and hardworking, some Krio banking professionals were ready to assist them in securing business loans to expand their private enterprises. It is doubtful, however, that Fulas would have received loans from Western banks, since they were often without valid immigration documents, and their long-term commitment to stay in Sierra Leone was in question. In addition, banks favored Lebanese, Indian, and European merchants for credit privileges. From a long-term perspective, both of these factors constrained Fula capital growth.[32]

In contrast to mercantile groups such as the Krio, Fula traders did not invest a significant amount of their profits in the higher education of their children abroad. It was a common practice among Krio traders to send their children to pursue law and medical studies in Britain. This practice required substantial investments, and the education thus obtained was perceived as prestigious and profitable. Paradoxically, it was a contributing factor to the commercial decline of the Krios, as Arthur Porter documents.[33] While a few wealthy Fula traders sent their children to undertake Islamic studies in Saudi Arabia, Senegal, Nigeria, and Mali, most of them were content to provide their children with rudimentary Islamic education in Sierra Leone or Guinea. Compared to the cost of overseas Western education, this Fula practice was inexpensive.

When the colonial period ended in 1961 the Fulas had already established themselves as an important mercantile group in Sierra Leone by successfully positioning themselves in key sectors of the economy. The decline of Krio merchants, who had long played a significant role in the country's commerce, and the gradual withdrawal of foreign capital created a vacuum that the Fulas would help to fill in the post-independence Sierra Leonean economy. They faced competition, however, from Lebanese traders, who were increasingly dominating merchant capital. Indeed, merchant capital remained a cornerstone of the Sierra Leonean economy into the post-colonial era.[34]

Fulas, both as immigrants and Sierra Leonean citizens, overcame marginality through hard work, risk-taking, and group organization based on kinship networks to become successful business owners in a colonial economy. In addition, the role of Islam was vital in shaping Fula business values in a Western colonial context. These issues will prove useful to researchers investigating the entrepreneurial history of Sierra Leone on a macro level. However, there are difficulties in reconstructing not just Fula but African entrepreneurial history in general. Poor record keeping, as well as the reluctance of individuals to reveal their financial standing and business transactions, are some of the many problems with which the researcher has to grapple in piecing together the business history of Fulas and Africans in general. Often, the available evidence does not yield to quantification, which is vital to the understanding of business history.

NOTES

1. See Allen M. Howard, "Trade and Islam in Sierra Leone, 18th–20th Centuries" in *Islam and Trade in Sierra Leone,* edited by Alusine Jalloh and David E. Skinner (Trenton, New Jersey: Africa World Press, in press); C. Magbaily Fyle, "Fula Diaspora: The Sierra Leone Experience" in *History and Socio-Economic Development in Sierra Leone,* edited by C. Magbaily Fyle (Freetown: Sierra Leone Adult Education Association, 1988): 101–123; M. Alpha Bah, "Fulbe Migration and Settlement in Koindu Among the Kissi of Sierra Leone," Ph.D. diss., Howard University, 1983; and Christopher Fyfe, *A History of Sierra Leone* (London: Oxford University Press, 1962).

2. For a detailed discussion of the Sierra Leone colonial economy, see Martin H. Y. Kaniki, "The Economic and Social History of Sierra Leone, 1929–1939," Ph.D. diss., University of Birmingham, 1972; and R. G. Saylor, *The Economic System of Sierra Leone* (Durham, N.C.: Duke University Press, 1967); also see A. G. Hopkins, *An Economic History of West Africa* (New York: Columbia University Press, 1973).

3. See N. A. Cox-George, *Report on African Participation in the Commerce of Sierra Leone* (Freetown: Government Printer, 1957); and M. Kelfala Kallon, *The Economics of Sierra Leonean Entrepreneurship* (Lanham, Md.: University Press of America, 1990).

4. See M. Adamu and A. H. M. Kirk-Greene, eds., *Pastoralists of the West African Savanna* (Manchester: Manchester University Press, 1986); and V. Azarya, *Aristocrats Facing Change: The Fulbe in Guinea, Nigeria, and Cameroon* (Chicago: University of Chicago Press, 1978).

5. See J. B. Riddell, *The Spatial Dynamics of Modernization in Sierra Leone: Structure, Diffusion, and Response* (Evanston, Ill.: Northwestern University Press, 1970); M. Harvey, "Implications of Migration to Freetown: A Study of the Relationship Between Migrants, Housing, and Occupation" *Civilizations,* 18 (1968): 247–67.

6. The Protectorate, which was declared by the British colonial administration over the Sierra Leone hinterland in 1896, is defined as the area outside of Freetown comprising the Northern, Eastern, and Southern Provinces.

7. For more information about the Fula presence in the Sierra Leone interior, see Bah, "Fulbe Migration and Settlement in Koindu Among the Kissi of Sierra Leone"; Fyle, "Fula Diaspora"; A. Wurie, "The Bundukas of Sierra Leone" *Sierra Leone Studies* 1 (Dec., 1953): 14–25; and C. Magbaily Fyle, *The Solima Yalunka Kingdom* (Freetown: Nyakon Publishers, 1979).

8. See W. R. Bascom, "The Esusu: A Credit Institution of the Yoruba" *Journal of the Royal Anthropological Institute* 82 (1952): 63–69.

9. See David E. Skinner, "Islam and Education in the Colony and Hinterland of Sierra Leone (1750–1914)," *Canadian Journal of African Studies,* 10 (1976): 499–520; Michael Banton, *West African City: A Study of Tribal Life in Freetown* (London: Oxford University Press, 1957).

10. See M. Saif'ud Deen Alharazim, "The Origin and Progress of Islam in Sierra Leone" *Sierra Leone Studies,* 21 (Jan., 1939): 13–26; B. E. Harrell-Bond, Allen M. Howard, and David E. Skinner, *Community Leadership and the Transformation of Freetown (1801–1976)* (The Hague: Mouton, 1978), 41–70.

11. Sierra Leone Archives (hereafter referred to as "SLA"), Colonial Secretary's Office (hereafter "CSO"), File: N/440/42, Governor to District Commissioners, Dec. 16, 1945.

12. The boundary between Sierra Leone and French Guinea was established in 1895 under the Anglo-French agreement.

13. SLA, CSO File: N/48/36, Nov. 8, 1943.

14. See C. Magbaily Fyle, *Commerce and Entrepreneurship: The Sierra Leone Hinterland in the Nineteenth Century,* Occasional Paper no. 2 (Freetown: Institute of African Studies, University of Sierra Leone, 1977).

15. See V. R. Dorjahn and C. Fyfe, "Landlord and Stranger: Change in Tenancy Relations in Sierra Leone," *Journal of African History,* 3 (1962): 391–97.

16. This title is used by Muslim men who have made the *hajj* (pilgrimage) to Mecca.

17. SLA, CSO File: N/115/40, 1945.

18. See Alusine Jalloh, *In Search of Profits: Muslim Fulas in Twentieth-Century Sierra Leone* (n.p., forthcoming).

19. See Alusine Jalloh, "*Alhaji* Momodu Allie: Muslim Fula Entrepreneur in Colonial Sierra Leone" in Jalloh and Skinner, eds., *Islam and Trade in Sierra Leone.*

20. See H. V. Merani and H. L. Van der Laan, "The Indian Traders in Sierra Leone," *African Affairs,* 78 (Apr., 1979): 240–50; H. L. Van der Laan, *The Lebanese Traders in Sierra Leone* (The Hague: Mouton, 1975).

21. *Alhaji* A. B. Tejan-Jalloh, interview with the author.

22. See Arthur T. Porter, *Creoledom: A Study of the Development of Freetown Society* (London: Oxford University Press, 1963); and Kaniki, "The Economic and Social History of Sierra Leone."

23. See Jalloh, *In Search of Profits.*

24. See H. L. van der Laan, *The Sierra Leone Diamonds: An Economic Study Covering the Years 1952–1961* (London: Oxford University Press, 1965).

25. For a discussion of *Alhaji* Barrie's diamond trade, see Alusine Jalloh, "Muslim Fula Merchants and the Motor Transport Business in Freetown, 1961–1978," in Jalloh and Skinner, eds., *Islam and Trade in Sierra Leone.*

26. See William Reno, *Corruption and State Politics in Sierra Leone* (Cambridge: Cambridge University Press, 1995); A. Zack-Williams, *Tributors, Supporters and Merchant Capital: Mining and Underdevelopment in Sierra Leone* (Vermont: Ashgate, 1995).

27. See Jalloh, *In Search of Profits.*

28. See Allen M. Howard, "The Role of Freetown in the Commercial Life of Sierra Leone," in *Freetown: A Symposium,* edited by C. Fyfe and E. Jones (Freetown: Sierra Leone University Press, 1968), pp. 38–64.

29. See Jalloh, *"Alhaji* Momodu Allie: Muslim Fula Entrepreneur in Colonial Sierra Leone."

30. See Jalloh, "Muslim Fula Merchants and the Motor Transport Business in Freetown, 1961–1978."

31. See R. A. A. Kumpayi, "The Livestock Industry in Sierra Leone," Bachelor's (Hons) thesis, Fourah Bay College, University of Sierra Leone, 1966.

32. See N. A. Cox-George, *Report on African Participation in the Commerce of Sierra Leone* (Freetown: Government Printer, 1957).

33. See Porter, *Creoledom,* pp. 112–18.

34. See Jalloh, *In Search of Profits.*

Slavery in Africa and the Transatlantic Slave Trade

JOSEPH E. INIKORI

After decades of neglect, slavery in Africa took the center stage in African historiography in the 1970s and 1980s. Suddenly there was a lot of excitement about the subject among European and North American historians and anthropologists, although, somewhat curiously, the then-vibrant schools of history on the African continent—in particular the Ibadan school in Nigeria—showed little interest. The excitement generated an impressive amount of empirical research into African socioeconomic institutions, which the researchers labelled "slavery." Historians studying slavery on other continents, especially in the New World, where the slave population comprised people of African descent, were surprised to be told that "there were certainly more slaves in Africa in the nineteenth century than there were in the Americas at anytime," and that

> The scholarship of the last twenty years [1970 to 1990] has demonstrated that the variety and intensity of servile relationships and methods of oppression that can be equated with slavery were probably more developed in Africa than anywhere else in the world at any period in history.[1]

Some of these researchers also claim that in 1897 the slave population of northern Nigeria alone was "certainly in excess of 1 million and perhaps more than 2.5 million people," and that "Northern Nigeria's slave system [was] one of the largest slave societies in modern history."[2]

But can we be certain that the institution studied by Africanists approximates that studied by historians of classical history, European history, Asian history, and New World history? As Claude Meillassoux has stressed, "Slavery, rigorously defined, may have universal characteristics, but its definition . . . must be generally accepted if a real discussion is to take place."[3] Certainly, the use of terms such as *slave* and *slavery* invites comparison, and students of slavery in Africa have not been insensitive to the need to compare. In general, they have compared the slaves they discovered in Africa with those of the Americas. While conceding that there were some differences, it is argued that enough similarities existed for the people they identify as slaves in Africa to approximate to the universal social category of slave and slavery.[4] It has even been argued that there were extensive slave plantations in many African regions comparable to New World slave plantations.[5]

A few scholars have expressed discomfort with this analytical thrust, which certainly characterizes the mainstream literature on the subject. Some have argued that the late nineteenth-century servile institutions in Africa did not approximate to slave or slavery, but, not finding what they consider an appropriate alternative term, they have reluctantly used both terms with quotation marks.[6] Others have employed terms such as *captives* or *serfs* without offering a convincing explanation for their use. Frederick Cooper has criticized this trend, pointing out that "the word 'slave' carries with it a bundle of connotations — all of them nasty. This has led some Africanists to use terms like 'adopted dependents,' 'captives,' or 'serfs' for a person whom others would call a slave." He adds:

> The first euphemizes a process that was based on violence and coercion; the second distracts from the various possible fates that befell people and their descendants once the act of capture was completed; and the third misrepresents the nature of dependence and the slave's relationship to the land.[7]

This intervention by Cooper seems to have silenced the few dissenters. Apart from one or two lonely voices, it has been business as usual in the study of slavery in Africa since the 1980s. Meillassoux has stated that the inclusion of non-slaves is responsible for the claim that slavery in Africa was mild or benign,[8] but apart from his very helpful effort to provide a universal definition, he has not shown which social categories to include or eliminate. Similarly, Joseph E. Inikori has complained of terminological looseness in the study of slavery in Africa,[9] yet has failed to show how to bring precision and discipline to the enterprise.

Such an exercise is attempted in this essay, which will present a comparative examination of servile social categories in medieval Europe and precolonial Africa. I contend that slavery and serfdom under the socioeconomic conditions of medieval Europe provide better comparative insights for a precise and disciplined study of servile institutions in precolonial Africa than the New World comparisons that have hitherto been conducted. The societies of medieval Europe were closer in all respects to those of precolonial Africa than were the New World slave societies, which were specifically organized for the large-scale production of commodities for an evolving capitalist world market. In addition, slavery once coexisted with other dependent social categories in pre-capitalist Europe, and the coexistence of slavery and non-slave servile categories has been carefully studied by students of European history.

Drawing on these studies, I will apply their methods of separating the various dependent social groups to the descriptive evidence on precolonial African servile categories, in order to determine which of them corresponds more closely to slavery or to serfdom or to some other category. For the exercise to be manageable, I have chosen two extreme geographical points in Europe: England to the extreme west and Russia to the extreme east. The exercise affords the opportunity to delve further into the old debate of the contribution of the transatlantic slave trade to the transformation of African servile institutions.

Slavery was first brought to England by the Romans, but their departure in 407 A.D. did not end slavery in that country. The chaos that followed the collapse of the Roman empire provoked slave raids and encouraged slavery in England and other parts of Europe. The Anglo-Saxons, from the Danish peninsula and the coast lands of northern Germany and Holland, raided England for slaves and eventually took over the country.[10] Many of the indigenous Celts were enslaved. After their settlement, the Anglo-Saxon kingdoms continued to fight among themselves and take captives. In consequence, slaves made up a large proportion of the population of Anglo-Saxon England.[11]

Slave raids and slave trading by various groups in the British Isles continued into the eleventh century, with Bristol as the main exporting port and Ireland a major export market. The Anglo-Saxon bishop of Worcester, who fought hard against the slave trade from England, lamented, "You might well groan to see the long rows of young men and maidens whose beauty and youth might move the pity of the savage, bound together with cords, and brought to market to be sold."[12] In the end, the conquest of the warring groups in Britain and Ireland by the Normans stopped the slave raids and the trade in captives. The Westminster Council of 1102 proclaimed that "no one is henceforth to presume to carry on that shameful trading whereby heretofore men used in England to be sold like brute beasts."[13]

But the Normans did not enact a law abolishing slavery in England. Slaves remained a statistically important part of the population. Based on the Domesday enumeration of 1086, it has been estimated that all categories of free peasants taken together constituted only 14 percent of the total population of rural England in 1086. Various categories of unfree peasants made up the remaining 86 per cent, of whom slaves were 10.5 per cent of the whole rural population and different groups of serfs accounted for 75.5 per cent.[14] Thus, over a period of several hundred years, slavery coexisted with other servile institutions in England. The disappearance of slavery was a long process, in which slaves were gradually converted to other dependent social categories.

This process of conversion has been examined in some detail by M. M. Postan in *The Famulus: The Estate Labourer in the XIIth and XIIIth Centuries* (1954). It started when Anglo-Saxon slaveholders, like their counterparts in the Frankish kingdoms, began to move their slaves, whether manumitted or not, into separate landholdings of their own. The new arrangement allowed them much freedom to cater for themselves and maintain households of their own, while continuing to render labor services to the lords in the cultivation of their estates. This new group of landholding dependent cultivators were distinguishable from their preexisting counterparts mainly in terms of the greater labor services they owed to the lords.

At the same time, however, the lords continued to hold other slaves directly in their estates. These were housed, fed, and clothed by the lords, and they spent most of their time working the latter's estates. As a recognition of the significant difference between these groups of dependent cultivators, contemporary practice and modern medievalists limited the application of the term *slave* to those directly resident on the lords' estates and completely maintained by them. The slaves enumerated in the Domesday Inquest of 1086 belonged to this category.[15]

The process of converting slaves to landholding dependent cultivators in England was completed in the twelfth century, but by this time the most recently converted groups were still somewhere between being slaves and fully settled landholding dependent peasants. Their holdings were small in size and had been carved out recently from the lords' estates.[16] They still spent the greater part of their time cultivating those estates, from which they earned much of their livelihood in food and money. In addition, like the fully settled dependent peasants, by law they were not free to move.[17] Postan refers to them as serf smallholders settled on servants' holdings; medieval sources refer to them as *bovarii* or *famuli*.

What happened in England in the twelfth century, according to Postan, was a wholesale conversion of the remnants of the slave class to *bovarii*. As he put it,

> a bovarius was a serf who possessed few rights or franchises denied to the late-Roman or German slaves, and whose greater independence resulted not so much from his superior status as from his separate holding and his life away from the lord's *curia* [estate]. It is in this physical separation that the key to the change must be sought. The smallholder was able to set up a family and have some inducement to exploit to the full the land of his holding.[18]

Postan insists that the smallholders settled on servants holdings, the *bovarii*, were not slaves:

> Twelfth-century *bovarii* were not slaves; and neither were the bulk of their Domesday namesakes. Twelfth-century *bovarii* were serfs, and the difference of status between slave and serf may have been very slight. Yet it is impossible wholly to identify medieval serfs with slaves without repudiating the accepted view of medieval serfdom as a condition intermediate (though of course far from equidistant) between those of slavery and freedom. Now and again the Domesday scribes, more especially those responsible for recording the Herefordshire entries, go out of their way to underline the difference between the *bovarius* and the slave.[19]

Thus, by contemporary practice and by the method of separation and classification adopted by medieval historians, there were several categories of serfs in England in the twelfth century. The common denominator for all of them was the possession of land, which they cultivated for themselves. Also linking them was the labor service they owed their lords and their lack of freedom to move under the law. They were, on the other hand, separated by the amount of labor dues they had to render, the amount of land they held, and the amount of time available to them to cultivate it. Serfs without slave origin, by local custom and tradition, had larger holdings and more time to cultivate them. For serfs of slave origin, the labor dues, the size of holdings, and the amount of time available to work them all tended to depend on the distance in time from their slave ancestors. On these differences, Postan observes:

> The services of a smallholder regularly employed as a *famulus* were, relative to his holding and rent, incomparably greater than the labour dues of an ordinary villein. . . . The latter, unlike the true manorial servant, was left enough time to work his own holding, and had enough substance to employ a servant himself if he needed one. There was no question of maintaining him and his family by the lord's plough-team, food and money. In economic fact he was still a customary tenant, discharging his labour obligations, while the full-time *famulus* . . . was a labourer working another man's land and deriving his livelihood wholly or in the main from his employer's wages.[20]

In order to place Postan's examination of England's case in the general context of medieval Europe, it is enough to refer to the summary statement by R. H. Hilton, who notes that the word *serf* comes from the Latin word *servus*, which in classical times meant "slave"; while in the early Middle Ages the word *slave* was derived from the ethnic term *Slav*. By this time the descendants of the slaves of the classical period and most of the slaves of the Dark Ages had been settled on separate holdings of their own and were *servi casati*. Many of the slaves still resident on their lords' estates were Slavonic captives acquired by the Germans in their eastward expansion and sold in the slave markets of Western Europe. Medieval historians, therefore, use both words to distinguish between the conditions of the two broad categories of dependent cultivators. As Hilton put it,

> Although some slaves in antiquity were by no means completely without property the distinction between slaves and serfs is based on the fact that, on the whole, slaves were the chattels of their master, employed as instruments of production in agriculture or industry, receiving food, clothing and shelter from the master and possessing nothing. . . . Some peasants were descended from the *coloni* of the late Empire, who . . . sank into serfdom under the heavy weight of the obligations imposed on them by the estate owners and the state. . . . Other peasants were descendants of full slaves, some of their ancestors having been slaves under the Roman Empire, others having been enslaved during the wars of the Dark Ages. What distinguished these serfs from their slave ancestors was, of course, the fact that they were now *servi casati*, provided with their own holdings from the landown-

er's estate. Other medieval peasant serfs were descended from free men who had entered into various forms of dependence under lords.[21]

Like England and the rest of Western Europe, slavery antedated serfdom in Russia. But, while in England slavery died out in the twelfth century and serfdom in the fifteenth, in Russia slavery remained alive up to the early eighteenth century and serfdom began its development only in the mid-fifteenth, to be abolished by state law in the 1860s. The enserfment of the Russian peasants was associated with the construction and expansion of the Russian state. Muscovy had been one of several Russian principalities up to the fifteenth century. In 1462 a Russian empire ruled by the Muscovite state was established. The creation of the Russian empire was accompanied by the rise of a powerful nobility. The size of this aristocracy and its capacity to dominate the peasantry grew *pari passu* with the geographical expansion of the empire and the power of the Russian tsar. As all this happened, the previously free Russian peasants increasingly lost their freedom. The development followed an observable historical sequence. In the first instance the peasants' general freedom was gradually curtailed in the second half of the fifteenth and the greater part of the sixteenth century. This was followed by a total prohibition of their right to move in the late sixteenth and early seventeenth centuries. Between the seventeenth century and the first half of the eighteenth, the changes were formally codified. Thereafter the conditions of the Russian serfs moved closer and closer to those of chattel slaves as the powerful nobles acted in total disregard of the law and tradition.[22]

Meanwhile the Russian *kholopy* (slaves) were being transformed into serfs. From the mid-fifteenth to the early eighteenth century the enserfed peasants coexisted with their older servile "cousins," the slaves. In the course of the seventeenth century, however, slaves and serfs gradually merged. The remnants of the slave class were moved into the rank of serfs by the tsar Peter I in 1723.[23] As to distinguishing the slaves from the serfs in the period during which they coexisted, Kolchin writes:

> The main distinction between kholopy [slaves] and serfs was that whereas the latter were usually self-supporting, growing their own food on allotted plots of land, the former were usually maintained by their owners; instead of living in a village with the peasants, they lived in or near their owners' residences.[24]

However, the conditions of the Russian serfs deteriorated considerably over time. The practice of selling and buying serfs by noblemen, which began in the second half of the seventeenth century, became generalized in the eighteenth. Kolchin states that in the course of the eighteenth century serfs were "bought and sold, traded, won and lost at cards."[25] Legally they remained serfs, however, and the Russian government made it clear that what was abolished by state law in the 1860s was serfdom, not slavery. In 1858, on the eve of emancipation, there were a total of 11.3 million male serfs (11,338,042). In 1795 the figure had been 9.8 million (9,787,802).[26] Assuming an equal proportion of female serfs, the totals come to 19.5 million in 1795 and 22.7 million in 1858. The literature has regularly referred to all of them as *serfs*.[27]

In the preceding examples the formula employed by students of European history to distinguish serfs and other dependent social categories from slaves incorporates unambiguous elements: first and foremost, the serfs or non-slave dependent people must possess a means of production (mainly land) large enough to provide an income to support a household with unproductive children and old members; second, they must have enough free time to produce for themselves, in order to realize the potential income from the employment of their means of production; third, they must be allowed to retain for their own use as they pleased the income realized; and fourth, their residences must be physically separated from those of their lords. On the other hand, for a dependent people to be classified as slaves, they must spend virtually their entire working day on their lords' estates — they may be allotted some plots, but the size, and the time available to work them, would be so limited that they would have to be fed, clothed, and housed by their lords; and their owners must be free, under the law and by tradition, to sell them to any buyer. I propose to apply this formula to the dependent social categories of precolonial Africa.

Incidentally, the pioneers of modern African historiography conducted a somewhat similar exercise more than three decades ago when they debated the issue of whether the concept of feudalism could be applied to any of the political systems in precolonial Africa. Some aspects of that debate are relevant for the present purpose. It is, therefore, appropriate to start with a summary of its major points.

Following efforts being made in the 1940s and 1950s to constitute a typology of political organizations in precolonial Africa, Jacques Maquet suggested in 1962 that "the feudal system deserves to be considered as an important type of political organization in traditional Africa."[28] He outlined the defining features of feudal regimes that should be considered in applying the feudal concept to Africa, noting that the concept was originally applied by historians of Europe to describe the main features of the dominant political regimes that existed in Europe between the ninth and thirteenth centuries. The defining features were, therefore, stated in accordance with the conceptions of feudalism employed by two broad groups of students of medieval European history: Marxists and non-Marxists. For non-Marxists the essential element of feudal regimes is the vassalage bond, while for Marxists, the distinguishing element is the relation of surplus extraction defined by a particular form of land ownership.[29]

Jack Goody criticized such attempts to apply the concept of feudalism to precolonial African regimes. He began with the problem of transferring to African history a term for which there are conflicting conceptions, citing an Anglo-Soviet discussion on feudalism in which the English speaker dwelt on military fiefs and the Russian participant concentrated on class relations of surplus extraction between lords and peasants. Goody concluded that "the core institution of feudal society is seen as vassalage associated with the granting of a landed benefit (fief), usually in return for the performance of military duties."[30] He also examined specific cases of the application of the concept to African societies. His summary of Potekhin's description of Asante is of particular interest:

> Potekhin writes that "Feudal land ownership constitutes the foundation of feudal relations." Land belongs to a restricted circle of big landowners, while the peasant pays rent or performs services for the right to cultivate his land. In Ashanti, he finds "the exclusive concentration of land in the hands of the ruling upper strata," together with the conditional land tenure and hierarchies of dependence "typical of feudal society."[31]

Goody did not question the factual accuracy of the description, but thought that defining feudalism in terms of the ownership of land was not appropriate.

Of all the cases cited and summarized by Goody, only that of Basil Davidson specifically touches upon the question of slavery in Africa. Davidson's main point was to show that African feudalism shared many common features with feudalism in medieval Europe. He pointed out that during the formative period of feudalism in the European Dark Ages slaves were gradually transformed into serfs, while in Africa strong states and empires destroyed tribal equality and produced a mass of dependent people who were serfs and not slaves. Comparing Asante with England at the time of the Norman conquest, Davidson showed further similarities:

> Thus the titles and the rights of great lords, the obligations of the common people, the customs of trade and tribute, the swearing of fealty, the manners of war — all these and a hundred other manifestations have seemed to speak the same identical language of feudalism.[32]

Davidson seems to imply that slavery is incompatible with feudalism. For our present purpose, however, suffice it to say that we do not have to prove the existence of feudalism in order to establish the existence of serfs. Feudalism is a form of sociopolitical organization with several elements. At a given moment and place some elements may be present without others. Had Davidson been primarily concerned with the issue of slavery or serfdom in Africa, the right question to ask would have been whether the conditions of the people being considered approximated more closely those of serfs or those of slaves in medieval Europe.

However, these were not the issues queried by Goody whose main discomfort was with Davidson's tailoring of African history too tightly to European history. At the then stage of African historiography, Goody thought that African institutions should be studied in depth in their own right without attaching European labels. While encouraging comparative studies, he admonished African historians to stay clear of terms such as *tribalism, feudalism,* and *capitalism,* which invite crude comparison.[33]

J. H. M. Beattie concurred; in his study of Bunyoro in modern Uganda, he found that the political regime there contained three of the five features listed by Marc Bloch as defining feudalism in Europe. The missing elements were a special military class and evidence of the disintegration of a pre-existing strong state. Beattie concluded:

> Like Goody, I consider it to be more useful and illuminating to retain the term "feudalism" and its associated vocabulary for the complex European polities to which they were first applied (and perhaps to such other systems, like the Japanese one, which can be shown to resemble it in all or most of its essential features), and to describe the political Institutions of traditional Bunyoro and of other African kingdoms as far as possible in their own terms.[34]

It is a pity that the debate did not proceed further and examine in depth the issue of slavery and serfdom raised by Basil Davidson. Apparently it was concluded that these terms are to be avoided in the writing of African history, but this conclusion may be misguided. As will be shown shortly, slaves and serfs, properly defined, can be encountered in

African societies in specific periods and regions. The problem is how to distinguish them from each other and from other dependent social categories, and trace their historical development.

Let us now attempt to resolve this conundrum by applying the formula employed by historians of precapitalist Europe as outlined above. The main difficulty is the scantiness of descriptive evidence on the dependent social categories in question. However, the research of more than three decades has produced a reasonable amount of such evidence to make the exercise feasible. What is particularly important, this research has been most intensive in the geographical areas where dependent populations in precolonial Africa were mostly concentrated: the Western Sudan, the Sokoto Caliphate in the Central Sudan, and the East African Coast. These constitute the main focus of the exercise, but scattered evidence from other areas will be examined to provide the basis for a continental generalization. The late nineteenth century will provide a starting point, and then we will turn to the period before the transatlantic slave trade.

The dependent populations of the nineteenth-century Sokoto Caliphate of modern northern Nigeria were among the first groups of such populations in tropical Africa to be scientifically studied by modern scholars. In the late 1940s Michael Smith and his wife, Mary Smith, conducted an elaborate data collection on the socioeconomic conditions of the servile populations among the Hausa-Fulani in the northern parts of the Zaria emirate in the Sokoto Caliphate.[35]

Smith's descriptive evidence shows a hierarchical sociopolitical organization of the Zaria emirate. The population was distributed into two spatial locations: walled towns, which included the capital city of Zaria; and agricultural villages where the peasants lived, groups of which were located near each walled town. Administratively, the ruler of the emirate was the emir of Zaria, referred to as a king by Smith. Being part of the Sokoto Caliphate, he was answerable to the overall ruler of the Caliphate, whose seat was in Sokoto city. Assisting the emir in the administration of the emirate were fief-holding officials, all of whom resided in the capital city of Zaria. The walled towns and agricultural villages were held as personal fiefs by these officials, who appointed subordinate staff (*jekadu*) to oversee their administration. At the lowest level of authority, the agricultural communities were run by village chiefs. Several of these agricultural villages, known locally as *rinji* (plural, *rumada*), were made up of servile cultivators; Smith called them "slave-villages." They belonged mostly to the emir and his fief-holding officials residing in the capital city, although some also belonged to merchants and other non-office holders. Like the other villages, they had their own village chiefs.

The servile cultivators in the *rumada* lived in separate households, and possessed lands allotted to them by their lords. These were separate from the lords' fields and the harvests were retained by the servile peasants for the support of their households. In the mornings these dependent cultivators worked with their families on their own farms from the early hours to 9:30, at which time they went to their lords' fields. At midday the lords sent them food, and at 2:30 they were free to return to their own farms. Apart from the meal provided on the field, the servile cultivators were responsible for the maintenance of their households.

According to Smith, the dependent populations of Zaria were of two categories, the native-born *dimajo* (plural, *dimajai*) and those brought from outside by capture or by purchase. Those brought from outside could be sold, but the native-born could not be alienated. The latter "formed the main body of the military force, of the police, and of the administrative staff at a subordinate level."[36]

Polly Hill's study of Kano Emirate, one of the largest emirates in the Sokoto Caliphate (covering an area of over sixteen thousand square miles), adds further descriptive evidence. Of particular interest is the servile village belonging to the emir. A member of the village of servile descent, who was born in about 1885, told Hill in 1972 how the village had functioned in precolonial days:

> He said that in the early days there had been "about fifty" men and women slaves working on the land; that many were strangers who spoke poor Hausa; that they lived in separate houses they had built themselves, since there was no house corresponding to a *rinji;* that each slave was given a farm plot (*gayauna*) for his own use, a plot that could be inherited by a son (though not by a daughter) or lent to someone else (*aro*) but could not be sold. He said that the usual crops (grains, cassava, groundnuts, etc.) were grown on the main estate (*gandu*); that some slaves became rich enough to ransom themselves; that the slave households cooked or bought most of their own food, though during the farming season cooked meals were provided in the evening as well as on the farmland at midday; that the slaves were paid for any work (such as thatching) done for the Emir in the dry season; that some free men worked alongside the slaves . . .[37]

In general, Hill's description of the conditions of the servile populations in Hausaland complements Smith's evidence, although she is critical of some points. For example, she points out that the restriction on the sale of bonded people was not based on generational differences; rather, Hausa tradition and public opinion imposed severe limitations on the rights of masters to sell servile individuals living in a household. She further states that most bonded people in Hausaland lived in households "with their spouses and children, richer male slaves being polygynous."[38]

Another elaborate study of bonded populations in the Sokoto Caliphate is the one on the Bida emirate by Michael Mason, who describes how the Bida state, a unit of the Sokoto Caliphate, was established by a Fulani aristocratic family and expanded from 1857 to 1901. This expansion led to the subjugation of the Nupe, an indigenous population in the area that became the Bida emirate. Bida's military incursions into neighboring territories also brought captives from other ethnic groups, such as the Yoruba, Afenmai, Igbirra, and even the Hausa and Fulani. Both the subjugated Nupe populations and the captives brought from outside were settled in agricultural villages around Bida City, the capital of the emirate. These captive villages or settlements, known locally as *tungazi* (singular, *tunga*), numbered 55 by 1859; between 1859 and 1873, 694 new captive settlements were created; and by 1901 there were a total of 1,601 captive villages in the emirate. About two-thirds of them were settlements composed of subjugated indigenous Nupe populations. Mason believes that the total population of these villages must have been around 100,000 by 1901.[39]

The dwellers in these captive villages did not work collectively on their lords' fields, nor did they render any labor services. Rather, they produced entirely for themselves and paid tributes to their lords in cash (*cowries*) and in kind (farm products).[40] Mason calls them slaves, and their settlements, slave plantations. However, he points out:

> In Nupe, although slaves did not live together with the lineages of their owners, we do not see that the social relations between slaves and their masters were fundamentally different from the relations between the lords or *egbazi* (sing. *egba*) and the peasants who paid them tribute. Slaves and peasants both paid tribute. Otherwise, the slaves kept their own products.

He adds that there was only one social relation of production in nineteenth-century Nupe, "the one which we have called 'tributary.' This mode colored all relations between masters and slaves and between lords and peasants."[41]

Based on the descriptive evidence presented, how do we categorize the servile populations of the Sokoto Caliphate in the nineteenth century? We need to stress that the studies presented do not cover all the emirates of the caliphate, and that the extent to which the emirates studied are representative of the whole caliphate is not easy to say. These emirates do, however, adequately represent the ethnic composition of the caliphate: Kano Emirate (predominantly Hausa); northern Zaria (servile settlements studied were held mostly by the Fulani); and Bida Emirate (predominantly non-Hausa–Fulani). Whether the geographical location and the ethnic composition of the emirates affected the conditions of the servile populations is unclear; what is clear is that they were all involved primarily in agricultural production. It should also be noted that in all the emirates of the caliphate, members of the Fulani aristocracy were large holders of servile populations.

Having said this, it is possible to agree that in parts of the caliphate some newly acquired captives, by purchase or through capture, and some of those who lived within the residences of their masters lived and worked under conditions that approximated those of slavery. These would be the ones Jan Hogendorn refers to as unmarried slaves who were fed by their masters throughout the year.[42] (Certainly, unmarried members of servile households worked and ate with their parents.) Based on the evidence presented, it is clear that this category of dependent cultivators did not constitute a large proportion of the total servile population in the Sokoto Caliphate in the late nineteenth century. The vast majority were householders settled on holdings of their own and were, therefore, *servi casati*. They possessed enough land and had enough time and motivation to produce for themselves and maintain a household.[43] Both in status and in economic independence, most of them were superior to the *bovarii* of twelfth-century England. Many were in the category of the villein of medieval Europe, and, as Mason's work shows, the dwellers of the captive villages in Bida had greater economic independence than even the villeins of medieval Europe. What is more, the dwellers of the servile villages in the Sokoto Caliphate were superior in economic independence and social status to the nineteenth-century Russian serfs. Applying the formula employed by European historians to distinguish between slaves and serfs in precapitalist Europe to the evidence from the Sokoto Caliphate therefore leads to the conclusion that the bulk of the servile populations in the caliphate hitherto referred to as slaves by scholars were in fact *servi casati*, that is, serfs. To call the servile villages in Bida and other parts of the Caliphate "slave plantations," we would have to accept that the medieval manor in

England and the serf village in nineteenth-century Russia were all slave plantations.

In fact, several of the authorities cited above are uncomfortable with the use of the terms *slave* or *slavery* to describe the servile populations they studied. For example, Mason explains:

> I have used the term "slave" only because of its familiarity and its currency in discussions of unfree labour in African societies. As I have suggested in the title, "captive" is a more appropriate term, as it is principally the mode of recruitment which the West African "slave" had in common with his brother in Cuba or Brazil.[44]

While Hill writes:

> Unlike genuine chattel slaves in ancient Greece and Rome, in the United States, and in Brazil and Haiti, who were always totally devoid of rights, farm-slaves in rural Hausaland normally enjoyed so many rights (including those of self-ransom) that it is reasonable to ask whether the term slave is, in fact, an appropriate translation of the Hausa *bawa*. However, quite apart from the impossibility of finding any alternative English word, it is clear that present-day definitions . . . are sufficiently commodious to include the Hausa variant.

When a definition is too "commodious" it ceases to define anything, however, and Hill later complains: "So it seems that, after all, the use of the term 'slavery' does confuse certain essential issues in rural Hausaland and that a substitute ought to be coined."[45]

Michael Watts has also argued that the extent to which the upper classes in the Sokoto Caliphate depended on the surplus produced by slaves has been "implausibly inflated":

> In some of the northern and peripheral emirates, perhaps less than 10 percent of the populace was servile, and while Kano and Sokoto may have been high-density systems, we are after all referring to a society constituted by perhaps 8 to 10 million "free" peasants. . . . The rights of ownership and production that farm slaves possessed converged with the slaveholders' ideology of the Islamic patriarch, assimilation, and the possibility of manumission. In short, the political, economic, and ideological tendencies in the Caliphate were toward the *production of peasants* who, if not entirely free, could at least be taxed or retained in a quasi-client status.[46]

So, while some members of the servile population in the Sokoto Caliph-ate were approximately slaves, a more precise use of terms, in the man-ner of modern historians of precapitalist Europe, would compel scholars to describe the vast majority of them as serfs. In other words, what the British colonial administration ended in Northern Nigeria in the early twentieth century was more serfdom than slavery.

The evidence for the Western Sudan is similar in many ways to that of the Sokoto Caliphate. Martin A. Klein, who has written extensively on the servile populations of the region, describes how their labor was rationally exploited in the nineteenth century: "slaves were settled in separate villages or separate quarters and there was increasing control over labour, feeding and dues."[47] He points to two possible ways of grouping the populations: the native-born versus those acquired by pur-chase or by capture, and those who resided within their lords' com-pounds versus those who settled in separate villages. The native-born could not be sold, while many of those residing within their masters' compounds were newly acquired, along with some trusted retainers and concubines. The latter group were fed and clothed by their masters, and those settled in villages worked under chiefs of servile descent. As Klein reports, "the larger numbers and the relative autonomy" of those living in separate villages "made possible the development of leader-ship."[48]

The micro-studies by Marion Johnson and by William Derman pro-vide descriptive detail for the region. Johnson studied the state of Ma-sina, established by a Muslim teacher and his followers in the region generally referred to as the Niger Bend (including Timbuktu and areas to the west). The state was created in the early nineteenth century and lasted until the 1860s, when its capital was destroyed by Al-Hajj Umar. The process of establishing the state and expanding its geographical area created subjugated populations, referred to as *rimaibe* (singular, *di-madio*), some held by the state and others by private Fulani pastoralists. Many of these people were settled in villages and were given lands, with one-sixth of the harvest to be paid as rent; a quantity of grains was also paid in dues called *diamgal* (settlements held by the state paid only *di-amgal*). Johnson dismissed the suggestion that the settlement of the ser-vile populations in separate villages of their own was brought about by the founder of the Masina state, who transformed preexisting chattel slaves into serfs with defined rights:

> The Masina system is so similar to the arrangements in adjacent terri-tories which never came under control of the Masina theocracy, that

it seems more probable that Sheku Ahmadu [the founder of the Masina state] formalized and regulated a pre-existing system.[49]

Derman's study was conducted in the Fouta-Djallon area of the modern Republic of Guinea, where, in a Fulani-led *jihad* from about 1727, the indigenous Diallonke, Susu, and Poullis were conquered and reduced to servile status. The subjugated indigenous population and captives brought from outside were settled in villages, where they produced for themselves on lands rented from the Fulani overlords: "they were economically self-sufficient. They lived in their own villages, they cultivated their own fields and women's gardens (although they did not own the land), owned property and had their own kin groups."[50] The rent for the land was ten percent of the harvest. The servile cultivators often rented lands from their masters, but sometimes from other Fulani landowners. Apart from the rent, they owed their masters labor dues, working "five days a week for their masters from early morning until early afternoon." Although Derman contends that these people were reduced to poverty by the amount of labor demanded by their masters, the labor dues seem to be of about the same magnitude as those of Kano Emirate and Zaria in the Sokoto Caliphate. The fact that the servile population of the Fouta-Djallon grew naturally after French conquest ended the wars and stopped the supply of new captives is an indication that the servile cultivators produced enough from their lands to support households with unproductive children and old members.[51]

The servile villages also had a good amount of autonomy to look after their own affairs. For example, disputes in a village were settled by the elders, while political leadership was provided by a member whose master was a chief. This political leader was also the link between the servile village and the Fulani overlords.

Taking all the evidence together, we can agree with Klein that many of the newly acquired captives and some others in the nineteenth-century Western Sudan lived and worked under conditions that approximated those of slaves, but the majority of the servile population did not belong to this category. The evidence shows clearly that those in the servile villages were *servi casati* living in households and supporting themselves. These people constituted the majority of those in servitude in the region on the eve of French conquest.

We now come to servitude on the East Coast of Africa. Here, Frederick Cooper has studied servitude in four important locations: two islands, Zanzibar and Pemba, where Omani Arabs produced cloves on a large scale in plantations; and two towns on the mainland, Malindi and

Mombasa (both in modern Kenya), where Arabs, Swahili, and migrant Africans employed servile labor to produce grains for local and export markets. The evidence shows considerable differences in the socioeconomic conditions of the servile populations in these places. In the clove plantations of Pemba and Zanzibar, they lived in huts "scattered around the plantations, dispersed among the clove trees." The main tasks of the servile workers were harvesting, planting, and tending the young clove trees. There were two harvests each year, a large one in November or December and a smaller one from July to September. Planting, watering the young plants, and weeding were year-round tasks. During the harvest season, these servile cultivators worked eight or nine hours a day, seven days a week; at other times they worked five or six days a week. They were allotted some plots where they produced some of their own food, mostly cassava.[52]

In Malindi the servile cultivators worked in the grain fields of their masters in groups of five to twenty, under a headman of servile status. The work week was between forty and fifty hours. The cultivators were allotted small plots of between two hundred by ten yards and two hundred by fifty yards, where they produced some of their own food. During the dry season, Thursdays and Fridays were set aside for them to work their own plots, while in the wet season (the main agricultural season) they had only Fridays off. According to Cooper, "Most informants claimed that masters provided slaves with a daily ration of food and that the produce of the slaves' own plots was a supplement to this. Masters were also expected to provide their slaves with clothes."[53]

In Mombasa, on the other hand, servile cultivators held by several masters lived in villages of their own, each village containing from fifty to three hundred people. Some of them worked on their own and paid their masters a monthly or annual sum called *ijara*. Others cultivated the nearby fields of their masters without supervision; a quantity of grain was paid as rent to their town-dwelling masters, who periodically went to the villages to collect it. The dwellers of these servile villages around Mombasa were left with much autonomy. Cooper reports, "In the Mombasa area, slaves often lived in villages containing slaves owned by various masters. They were governed by a slave headman elected by their own elders. He was expected to arrest any suspected criminals and send them to Mombasa for trial."[54]

Taking the evidence together, we agree entirely with Cooper that the servile cultivators of the clove plantations and in mainland Malindi can accurately be referred to as slaves. Even though they had some small plots allotted to them, they did not have enough time to produce for

themselves and maintain a reasonable level of socioeconomic independence. The small size of the plots, less in area than a soccer field, is
itself indicative. Although the demographic evidence is scanty, it clearly
indicates that the servile populations in the clove plantations did not
reproduce themselves socially, in spite of the favorable gender balance.
The observation of contemporary visitors that the rate of reproduction
was low and the death rate high is consistent with the hard data showing
that mainland-born people were two-thirds of the servile population
in 1900–1901. Since large-scale slave imports from the mainland were
concentrated in the first four decades of the nineteenth century, as the
growth of clove exports suggests, a reasonable reproduction rate should
have given rise to a much greater proportion of island-born people in
the population by this time.[55] This demographic evidence points further
to the low level of socioeconomic autonomy among the servile populations of the clove plantations.

The case of those in the mainland area of Mombasa is a different
matter. There we are dealing with people whose socioeconomic autonomy was greater than that of even the villiens in medieval Europe, not
to mention that of the *bovarii* of twelfth-century England and the serfs
of nineteenth-century Russia. It is an inexcusable terminological looseness to lump together the dependent cultivators of the Mombasa area
and the servile populations of Malindi, Zanzibar, and Pemba under the
same dependent social category. The former certainly resembled serfs
more than slaves.

Having examined the regions with high densities of servile populations in precolonial Africa, it is tempting to generalize that nothing very
different existed in other regions. That may well be the case in places like
Asante, Dahomey, and the Benin kingdom of south-western Nigeria. In
such places, a significant population of dependent people whose socioeconomic conditions approximated slavery existed side by side with
others, greater in number, whose conditions were closer to those of
serfs. There are regions, however, in which the people described as
slaves by scholars had so much freedom that it would not be appropriate
even to call them serfs, as in the case of the Puna and Kuni societies of
modern Congo, where the so-called slaves labored in the same way as
their free counterparts, could hold any office in their society, and were
usually married to free spouses from the lineages of their masters.[56]
There is also the interesting case of the servile warriors of Mozambique
in the period from 1825 to 1920, who more resemble the knights of medieval Europe: they lived in their own villages, scattered all over the
land; they had their own leaders, appointed from among them by their

masters; and they constituted the instruments with which the lordly class dominated the peasants, collecting tribute from the peasants and imposing discipline on the peasant communities. The most important service they rendered to their masters, however, was military.[57]

Thus, it is factually correct to say that a significant number of people in late nineteenth-century Africa south of the Sahara labored under socioeconomic conditions approximating slavery. However, it is also factually correct to say that the numbers of such people have been grossly exaggerated by scholars. Most of the people usually described as slaves were in fact not slaves at all. By the yardstick employed by historians of precapitalist Europe to separate slaves from serfs, the bulk of these people were serfs; indeed, some were free people.

If we can agree that a significant number of slaves existed in parts of sub-Saharan Africa in the late nineteenth century, was this also true of the pre-transatlantic slave trade period? To answer this question we must turn to the socially stratified societies with established centralized state systems in the Western Sudan and in West-Central Africa. The agrarian societies of the fifteenth and sixteenth centuries, which subsequently formed the nucleus of the Asante state, should also be examined, for it is known that Asante economic and political entrepreneurs purchased captives from other African regions at this time.

The accounts of the first Europeans to come into contact with West African societies in the Western Sudan (the Senegambia area) do contain references to dependent social categories that these Europeans classified as slavery. Studies based on Arabic sources indicate that those sources also contain references to slaves in the societies of the Western Sudan. The combined authority of the Arabic and early European sources gave rise to the generally accepted view that the impact of the trans-Saharan trade occasioned the widespread use of slaves to produce commodities and to provision the aristocracy and state functionaries in the Western Sudan long before the first Europeans arrived on the West African coast.[58] As more detailed description of the material conditions of the populations referred to in these sources as slaves becomes available, it appears that historians have been too uncritical of the sources in question.

From what we know of the history of the Western Sudan from the beginning of the present millennium to the end of the sixteenth century, Songhay was the largest and most complex state system that ever existed in the region before the coming of the first Europeans. It was heavily involved in the trans-Saharan trade and exhibited a highly developed class system. If there was an extensive use of slaves in the region, the

Songhay of the twelfth to the sixteenth century must be the place to find them in large numbers. S. M. Cissoko holds that indeed there were many slaves in Songhay. Based on the terminology employed in the Arabic sources, he says that private and state officials of Songhay employed large numbers of slaves to cultivate their estates in the rural areas, but his descriptive evidence tells a different story. This can be best observed in Cissoko's own words:

> Large estates belonging to the princes and *ulamas* of the great towns were worked by slaves, settled in farming villages. The askiya was himself one of the great landowners. His fields, scattered throughout the valley, were cultivated by communities of slaves working under overseers called *fanfa*. A sort of rent in kind was levied on the harvests and sent to Gao. The same happened with private slaves.[59]

He adds further details:

> The *Ta'rikhs* give us a few glimpses of country life. There is virtually no mention of peasants' revolts. The rent demanded from the slaves by their masters was never crushing. . . . The peasants even sold part of their produce in the local markets, obtaining products like salt or cloth and thus becoming involved in trade.[60]

The descriptive evidence leaves no doubt that we are dealing with landowning servile cultivators, producing for themselves and paying rent to their town-dwelling lords. They were located in villages and physically separated from their lords. The fact that the rent demanded "was never crushing" must mean that the dependent peasants could maintain households with unproductive children and old members and therefore were able to reproduce themselves socially. D. T. Niane concludes that these dependent peasants were serfs and not slaves:

> Up to the present time [12th–16th century] in black Africa, before the monetary economy developed, land was considered to be the indivisible property of the community. The kings and emperors had "human estates," that is, lands worked by subjugated communities; but closer examination shows that this was a system of serfdom rather than slavery.[61]

It is possible that some slaves did exist in the Western Sudan by the fifteenth century, but newly available evidence indicates that the literature on the subject stands in need of revision. The descriptive evidence in the sources should be carefully reexamined in order to separate true slaves, if any, from serfs and other dependent social categories.

If it is hard to find true slaves in the societies affected by the trans-Saharan trade before the coming of the Europeans, it is even harder to do so in the coastal societies of Western Africa and their hinterlands, which were not directly affected by that trade. Somehow, Asante occupied a borderland between the societies of the Western Sudan that were directly involved in the trade and those farther down the Atlantic coast, which only received indirect effects. In fact, Asante economic and political entrepreneurs, who accumulated wealth from the sale of gold to the merchants of the Western Sudan, bought captives in the fifteenth and sixteenth centuries to clear virgin lands for agriculture. Some of the captives came from the Western Sudan; others were imported from the Benin kingdom by the Portuguese and sold to the Asante entrepreneurs. This situation prompted some historians to argue that Asante already had a slave class by the fifteenth century. However, Ivor Wilks has now shown that the purchase of people by the Asante in the fifteenth and sixteenth centuries did not produce a slave class at that time. The wealthy Asante, who bought people to clear the forests, took pains to avoid the creation of a slave class. The matriclan institution was invented at this time for this particular purpose. Wilks expressed that:

> One of the major thrusts in Asante social "engineering" was towards prevention of the consolidation of a slave caste: those of unfree origins were assimilated as rapidly as possible into the class of free Asante commoners and their acquired status afforded full protection of the law. . . . But the precise way in which such task forces were incorporated and assimilated into the open-textured matriclans must remain for the present a matter for speculation; all that is sure is that incorporation and assimilation occurred, and that in consequence no slave caste arose within Asante society.[62]

Therefore, to the extent that there were slaves in Asante in the nineteenth century, their origin must be associated with conditions created after the coming of the Europeans.

The other major region where recent research has produced helpful evidence on social structure before the transatlantic slave trade is West-Central Africa. This region is important, because it was not involved in the trans-Saharan trade, and it was one of the early major suppliers of slaves to the European traders. When Europeans arrived in the late fifteenth century, the Kingdom of Kongo, the main centralized state system in the region, was continuing its territorial expansion. Its political economy rested on the collection and redistribution of tribute products from different ecological regions of the state. As the kingdom expanded geographically, the range of tribute products increased and the income of the ruling elites came to depend on the tributes.[63]

This early tribute system apparently eliminated the need for production by slaves to support the rulers. There were political clients, servants, and prisoners of war, but no slave class; there was no trade in people of any type before the coming of the Portuguese. Hence, there was no word for slave or slavery among the pre-contact Kongo people. Anne Hilton states that as late as the seventeenth century "the only term which referred to purchase [that is, purchased people], *muntu a kusumbira*, was a compound construction suggesting that the phrase had been devised to express a new condition."[64]

Jan Vansina's elaborate linguistic study of West-Central Africa corroborates the conclusions derived primarily from archival sources. On the basis of linguistic evidence, Jan Vansina has stated that there was no trade in people in the region before the coming of the Europeans, and that the various words meaning "slave" in the region are "loanwords" that evolved as the European slave trade spread from the coast into the interior. In particular, Vansina studied in detail the etymology of the term, *-pika*, which in Kongo meant "servant" before 1500, but later came to mean the traded "slave" in the major communities of Central Africa involved in the transatlantic slave trade.[65]

It is thus incorrect to say that the preexistence of widespread slavery in the coastal societies of Western Africa made possible the growth of the transatlantic slave trade. In a recent effort to revive this outdated explanation, John Thornton argues that African legal systems, which prevented private ownership of land, gave rise to the accumulation of slaves everywhere in Africa, and the transatlantic slave trade "was the outgrowth of this internal slavery." Based on a misunderstanding of medieval European history, Thornton argues that "by contrast, in European legal systems, land was the primary form of private, revenue-producing property, and slavery was relatively minor."[66] In fact, a careful examination of the evidence points to a considerable similarity between the land tenure system in the major states of medieval Europe and that in the major states of precolonial Africa. As Douglass North and Robert Thomas have pointed out, "Feudal law [in Europe] did not recognize the concept of land ownership,"[67] and Goody makes the same point:

> from the evidence concerning the inheritance of land at the village level [in medieval England] it would seem that here the idea that conquest put all rights in the hands of the Norman conquerors was some-

thing of a fiction. Whatever the legal position on this abstract level, the medieval system in practice appears to display some similarities with African land tenure, especially in states like Nupe.[68]

It was the same process which changed slaves and serfs to free peasants, as feudalism collapsed in Europe, that also gradually transformed the European feudal lord into a modern landlord.[69] It should be noted that when the market conditions in Africa were right in the nineteenth and twentieth centuries, no "African legal systems" could hold back the development of modern private property rights in land.

The evidence clearly refutes the contention that the transatlantic slave trade sprang from previously accumulated slaves in Africa. There was no process in place that regularly generated people for sale in the coastal societies of Western Africa before the coming of the Europeans. On the contrary, it was the power of European demand for captives to be exported as slaves that provoked large-scale gathering of captives for sale, which ultimately established a permanent process with supporting socioeconomic and political structures. One part of the socioeconomic structure was a large servile population, including slaves and serfs.

The best region to illustrate this argument is West-Central Africa, and the best case in the region is the Kingdom of Kongo. This kingdom had never been involved in a trade in people, but it had the capacity to generate captives from outside the polity, and these captives could be sold if conditions made that the best alternative, economically and politically, for the kingdom's economic and political entrepreneurs. To start, it should be noted that the main initial Kongo trade with the Portuguese was in copper. It was about thirty years after their arrival that the Portuguese shifted their emphasis from copper to slaves. Even by this time the King of Kongo had no immediately available "disposable people" to sell when the King of Portugal sent a trade mission to prepare the way for large-scale slave exports. As Hilton reports, while the Kongo ruler accepted the new trading arrangement and the gifts from the King of Portugal, he had no slaves to send even as return gifts:

> There were in fact very few slaves available for purchase and scarcely any had so far been exported from Kongo. In order to secure the return gift Afonso [the reigning King of Kongo] had to raid the neighboring Mbundu . . . newly acquired captives being the only people who could, at this time, be legitimately sold.[70]

Thus, during the early years (up to the second decade of the sixteenth century), when the slave trade remained marginal and while copper and cloth were dominant, not even the King of Kongo "had a large retinue of slaves,"[71] let alone the title-holders and provincial governors under him. At that time the kingdom did not even have a standing army. In the course of the sixteenth century, however, the sociopolitical and military conditions associated with the transatlantic slave trade led to the accumulation of dependent populations in Kongo. We do not know enough about their conditions. The literature refers to all of them as slaves; we can only guess that many were approximately slaves and others serfs.

The state was eventually forced to establish a standing army made up predominantly of slaves. Alvaro II (1587–1614) had sixteen to twenty thousand Tio slave guards. Officeholders and merchants in the capital city and other trading centers employed many servile people in agriculture to meet their subsistence needs. In the course of the seventeenth century the holding of servile cultivators in the central region of the kingdom became so widespread that almost every aggrieved person demanded slaves as compensation.[72]

The Kongo evidence shows that transatlantic slave exports developed without any assistance from a preexisting slave class. It also shows that political clients, servants, and other dependent peoples in precontact Kongo could not be sold by law and tradition. What is more, there is no indication that the rulers had a pathological drive for the accumulation of people as an end in itself, as is often claimed. On the contrary, these rulers, like rulers in all precapitalist societies, saw people as potential producers and subjects. Their attitudes were influenced by political expediency and the relative value of production factors in the short run, as determined by market opportunities.

No one who knows the response of African political and economic entrepreneurs to European demand for agricultural and other products in the nineteenth and twentieth centuries will be surprised by this finding. Western Africans never produced or traded cocoa and rubber before the coming of the Europeans, but when the latter demanded those products and were willing to pay prices that made their production rewarding, they were produced in rapidly growing quantities, although there was no previous experience to fall back on. Given the circumstances of African states in the era of the transatlantic slave trade, it is not hard to imagine that the political and economic value of European trade missions, like the one sent by the Portuguese to Afonso I of Kongo in 1512, must have been easy to sell to the rulers of those states, since they could procure the captives from outside their polities at very little cost to themselves.

We owe a significant intellectual debt to the historians and anthropologists who have studied slavery in Africa for the past two decades or so. Their research has helped to call attention to social and economic issues in the study of African history after the initial emphasis on political questions. However, the sociology of knowledge that directed the research seems to have encouraged a lack of attention to terminological precision. As we know too well, slavery in Africa was a major theme constructed by the European slave traders to defend their business against the abolitionist onslaught in the eighteenth century. The same theme also became fashionable for the agents of European colonialism in the late nineteenth and early twentieth centuries, as the abolition of slavery was presented to the moral conscience of Europeans as a part of the European "civilizing mission" to Africa. The propaganda by the slave traders and by the agents of colonialism was so effective that it was given intellectual respectability in history textbooks. One part of the propaganda — the claim that the preexistence of widespread slavery in Africa gave rise to and helped to sustain the transatlantic slave trade — was challenged in the mid–1960s by Walter Rodney.[73] It is fair to say that the subsequent encounter between Rodney and Fage set the stage for the research of the 1970s and 1980s on servile institutions in precolonial Africa. Even Rodney, however, while questioning the existence of slavery in the coastal societies of Western Africa before the transatlantic slave trade, accepted uncritically the colonial propaganda that slavery was everywhere in late nineteenth-century Africa.

Given the sociology of knowledge that informed the study of slavery in Africa, it is understandable why very little attention has been paid to terminological precision, which characterizes the study of dependent social categories in the history of precapitalist Europe. I have attempted to redress this weakness in the literature by applying to the African evidence the formula employed by modern historians to separate slaves from serfs in precapitalist Europe. The result shows that, while there were slaves in late nineteenth-century Africa, the bulk of the people hitherto so described more closely resembled serfs. The phenomenon of what scholars refer to as inter-generational mobility among the slave populations in Africa[74] — the tendency for the children of slaves to become free persons or nearly so — meant that the slave class in Africa could not reproduce itself, not only because its rate of reproduction was low, but largely because the children of slaves normally did not remain in slavery; they either became free or became serfs. Apart from the clove plantations of East Africa, most of what scholars have called "slave plantations" in Africa were, in fact, serf villages. To accept them as slave plantations, we must also accept the medieval manors in Europe and the serf villages of nineteenth-century Russia as slave plantations. In that case, Russia would have possessed the largest concentration of slaves in the nineteenth century, with over 22 million of them.

The evidence also shows that there were no slaves in the coastal societies of Western Africa in the fifteenth century to provide the springboard for the transatlantic slave trade. It is, therefore, misleading to speak of "transformations in slavery" in Africa from the fifteenth century.[75] What happened in the coastal societies of Western Africa and their hinterlands after the fifteenth century, following the socioeconomic and politico-military conditions associated with the transatlantic slave trade, was the transformation of free peasants, political clients, servants, and quasi-serfs into slaves and serfs. Following the worthy accomplishments of the research of the last two decades, what is needed now is terminological precision. We need to find ways of separating slaves from other dependent social categories in precolonial Africa and reinterpret the evidence.

NOTES

1. Paul E. Lovejoy, "Foreword," in Claude Meillassoux, *The Anthropology of Slavery: The Womb of Iron and Gold,* translated by Alide Dasnois (Chicago: University of Chicago Press, 1991), p. 7. Lovejoy's view is totally contrary to Meillassoux's argument in the book, which unambiguously states that tropical Africa was the last region in the world to develop a trade in slaves and the institution of slavery, many centuries after similar developments in Europe and Asia and around the Mediterranean (pp. 20–21).

2. Paul E. Lovejoy and Jan S. Hogendorn, *Slow Death For Slavery: The Course of Abolition in Northern Nigeria, 1897–1936* (Cambridge: Cambridge University Press, 1993), pp. xiii, 1.

3. Meillassoux, *The Anthropology of Slavery,* p. 22.

4. Martin A. Klein, "The Study of Slavery in Africa," *Journal of African History,* 19, no. 4 (1978): 599–609; Frederick Cooper, "The Problem of Slavery in African Studies," *Journal of African History,* 20, no. 1 (1979): 103–25; Paul E. Lovejoy, "The Characteristics of Plantations in the Nineteenth-Century Sokoto Caliphate (Islamic West Africa)," *American Historical Review,* 84, no. 5 (1979): 1267–92.

5. Paul E. Lovejoy, "Plantations in the Economy of the Sokoto Caliphate," *Journal of African History,* 19, no. 3 (1978): 341–68; Lovejoy, "The Characteristics of Plantations."

6. Igor Kopytoff and Suzanne Miers, "African 'Slavery' as an Institution of Marginality," in *Slavery in Africa: Historical and Anthropological Per-*

spectives, edited by Suzanne Miers and Igor Kopytoff (Madison: University of Wisconsin Press, 1977).

7. Cooper, "The Problem of Slavery," p. 105.

8. Claude Meillassoux, "Female Slavery," in *Women and Slavery in Africa,* edited by Claire C. Robertson and Martin A. Klein (Madison: University of Wisconsin Press, 1983). Meillassoux states that "one approach to African slavery, which stresses its benevolent character by comparison to American or West Indian slavery, tends to play down the differences between slaves and other dependent or dominated social categories, such as pawns, serfs, or even married women" (p. 50).

9. Joseph E. Inikori, *The Chaining of a Continent: Export Demand for Captives and the History of Africa South of the Sahara, 1450–1870* (Mona, Jamaica: Institute of Social and Economic Research, 1992), p. 37.

10. David Pelteret, "Slave Raiding and Slave Trading in Early England," in *Anglo-Saxon England,* vol. 9, edited by Peter Clemoes (Cambridge: Cambridge University Press, 1981), pp. 99–114. Pelteret writes: "In contrast to the Roman world, slavery seems not to have been an integral element in the social structure of the Germanic peoples living outside the Empire at the time when Tacitus was writing about them" (p. 100). But the Anglo-Saxons were involved in taking captives and exporting them to places in the Roman empire before they moved into England. That practice of taking and selling captives continued for centuries after they settled in England.

11. Pelteret, "Slave Raiding," pp. 99, 102.

12. *Life of St. Wulstan, Bishop of Worcester,* translated by J. H. F. Peile (Oxford, 1934), pp. 64–65, cited by Pelteret, "Slave Raiding," p. 113, n. 107.

13. *Eadmer's History of Recent Events in England,* translated by G. Bosanquet (London: University of Wisconsin Press, 1964), p. 152, cited by Pelteret, "Slave Raiding," p. 113, n. 111.

14. H. E. Hallam, "England before the Norman Conquest," in *The Agrarian History of England and Wales: Volume II, 1042–1350,* edited by Hallam (Cambridge: Cresset Press, 1988), pp. 10–12. In *The Famulus: The Estate Labourer in the XIIth and XIIIth Centuries* (London: Cambridge University Press, 1954), M. M. Postan has suggested that the percentage of slaves in the total population may have been less than the Domesday figures imply: "Corrected by the coefficients which historians employ to translate the Domesday figures of households into numbers of heads, the proportions of slaves to the total Domesday population would probably turn out to be smaller than the gross figures in the Domesday might suggest. For we must assume that whereas a large proportion of the slaves were not in a position to establish families, all the other social groups were counted in family units" (pp. 5–6).

15. Postan holds that by 1086 the conversion process had not gone far

enough to engulf "that portion of the slave class whom lords were still employing in their *curia*" (Postan, *The Famulus,* p. 11).

16. Postan, *The Famulus,* pp. 12–13.

17. Ibid., p. 23.

18. Ibid., p. 36. Earlier in the work, Postan had stated: "How fundamental the change-over from slave to *bovarius* was, is not a question to which a simple answer is possible. It may have signified nothing more than a modification of their status, and may not have been of very great economic importance. On the other hand it may have been one of habitation — the resident slave may have been transformed into a land-holding servant — in which case it was of great economic significance" (p.11).

19. Ibid., p. 9.

20. Ibid., p. 25. This way of looking at slavery and serfdom would seem to be consistent with Meillassoux's theoretical construct, which distinguishes slavery from serfdom on the basis of the dependent producer's capacity to retain a proportion of his surplus large enough to raise a family and maintain a household. Under Meillassoux's framework, if the dependent producer possessed enough land and had enough time to work it and keep a surplus large enough to raise children and maintain old members of the household, then he was a serf. On the other hand, if the lord's demand for surplus labor was so great that the dependent producer was unable to maintain a household, then he was a slave. Hence, the observation that in all slave systems the slave class is unable to reproduce itself socially, being born of the "womb of iron and gold" — capture by force of arms and purchase with money on the market. See Meillassoux, *The Anthropology of Slavery.*

21. R. H. Hilton, *The Decline of Serfdom in Medieval England* (London: Macmillan, 1969), pp. 9–11.

22. Peter Kolchin, *Unfree Labor: American Slavery and Russian Serfdom* (Cambridge, Mass.: The Belknap Press of Harvard University Press, 1987), pp. 2–4, 41. The discussion of the Russian serfs is based largely on Kolchin's work.

23. Ibid., pp. 2–3.

24. Ibid., pp. 37–38.

25. Ibid., p. 43. By the mid-eighteenth century there were two broad groups of peasants, state peasants and serfs. The latter, owned almost exclusively by noblemen, constituted over fifty percent of the peasant population. The state peasants were made up of those who escaped enserfment and those recently freed (Ibid., p. 39).

26. Ibid., p. 52. It is not clear whether male serfs refers to heads of household or to all males, including children. If reference is to heads of household, then the total serf population was much greater than what is stated here.

27. Historians have debated the issue of whether the nineteenth-century Russian serfs were actually slaves or serfs in the main, although their conditions came close to those of chattel slaves. This is an important distinction, contrary to the view of Kolchin, who thinks that the dispute is mere hairsplitting. The sale of the serfs certainly moved them very close to chattel slaves. But, as Kolchin himself acknowledged, most serfs continued to receive allotments of land of their own from their owners with which they supported themselves (*Ibid.*, pp. 43–45). For this reason they were *servi casati,* and the demographic evidence indicates that they were able to maintain a household and reproduce themselves socially. Their sale was also regulated by state laws: Peter I decreed in 1721 that family members must not be separated by sale; and in the nineteenth century Nicholas I twice outlawed the selling of unmarried children away from their parents (Ibid., p. 117). It is fair to say that in the main these people were serfs, but over time their conditions came close to those of chattel slaves.

28. Jacques J. Maquet, "A Research Definition of African Feudality," *Journal of African History,* 3, no. 2 (1962): 307.

29. Maquet thought that the Marxist conception would be difficult to apply to precolonial Africa, where the notion of land ownership embodied in Roman law was non-existent. See Maquet, "African Feudality," p. 309.

30. Jack Goody, "Feudalism in Africa?," *Journal of African History,* 4, no. 1 (1963): 3.

31. Goody, "Feudalism in Africa?," p.10. He refers to I. I. Potekhin's "On the Feudalism of the Ashanti," a paper read to the Twenty-fifth International Congress of Orientalists in Moscow (1960).

32. Basil Davidson, *Black Mother: The Years of the African Slave Trade* (Boston: Atlantic Monthly Press, 1961), pp. 11–12.

33. Goody, "Feudalism in Africa?," pp. 10–13. Goody may as well have included words like *slavery* and *plantations.*

34. J. H. M. Beattie, "Bunyoro: An African Feudality?," *Journal of African History,* 5, no. 1 (1964): 26, 35.

35. See Mary F. Smith, ed., *Baba of Karo: A Woman of the Muslim Hausa,* with introduction and notes by Michael G. Smith (London: Faber and Faber, 1954); Michael G. Smith, "A Study of Hausa Domestic Economy in Northern Zaria," *Africa,* 22, no. 4 (1952): 333–47; M. G. Smith, "Slavery and Emancipation in Two Societies," *Social and Economic Studies,* 3, no. 3–4 (Dec., 1954): 239–90; and M. G. Smith, *Government in Zazzau, 1800–1950* (London: Oxford University Press, 1960).

36. Smith, "Slavery and Emancipation," pp. 244, 253, 264–267; Smith, *Government in Zazzau,* pp. 86, 89–90; Smith, introduction to *Baba of Karo,* p. 22.

37. Polly Hill, "From Slavery to Freedom: The Case of Farm-Slavery in Ni-

gerian Hausaland," *Comparative Studies in Society and History*, 18, no. 3 (1976): 418.

38. Ibid., pp. 402–404.

39. Michael Mason, "Captive and Client Labour and the Economy of the Bida Emirate, 1857–1901," *Journal of African History*, 14, no. 3 (1973): 459–60.

40. Mason, "Captive and Client Labour," pp. 465–68.

41. Michael Mason, "Production, Penetration, and Political Formation: The Bida State, 1857–1901," in *Modes of Production in Africa: The Precolonial Era,* edited by Donald Crummey and C. C. Stewart (Beverly Hills: Sage Publications, 1981), pp. 214–15.

42. Jan Hogendorn, "The Economics of Slave Use on Two 'Plantations' in the Zaria Emirate of the Sokoto Caliphate," *International Journal of African Historical Studies,* 10 (1977): 378.

43. According to the more detailed work schedule presented by Hogendorn, the dependent cultivators in Zaria rose by 4:00 A.M. for the morning prayer, after which they went with their families to their own farms. At 9:00 A.M. they moved to their lords' fields and worked until midday, when they rested and had their meals. By 2:00 P.M. work on the lords' fields was over and they were free to return to their own farms. This schedule was followed during the farm season, which lasted (including the harvesting period) probably no more than six or seven months. During the dry season, from November to April, they worked mostly for themselves and were paid when they worked for their lords. See Hogendorn, "The Economics of Slave Use," pp. 375–76; and Hill, "From Slavery to Freedom," p. 418. Assuming that the morning prayers lasted an hour, the servile cultivators must have had at least six hours daily to devote to their own farms during the farming season (allowing for movement to and from the lords' fields), while spending at most about four hours on their lords' fields. Of course, there was a lot of time during the dry season to engage in non-agricultural activities for themselves: hunting, handicraft production, and so on.

44. Mason, "Captive and Client Labour," p. 453, n. 2.

45. Hill, "From Slavery to Freedom," pp. 397, 413.

46. Michael Watts, *Silent Violence: Food, Famine and Peasantry in Northern Nigeria* (Berkeley: University of California Press, 1983), pp. 77–78. Despite this telling criticism, Watts still talks of "several million slaves" in the Sokoto Caliphate in the late nineteenth century (p. 191).

47. Klein, "The Study of Slavery," p. 607.

48. Martin A. Klein, "Slave Resistance and Slave Emancipation in Coastal Guinea," in *The End of Slavery in Africa,* edited by Suzanne Miers and Richard Roberts (Madison: University of Wisconsin Press, 1988), pp. 208–209.

49. Marion Johnson, "The Economic Foundation of an Islamic Theocracy — The Case of Masina," *Journal of African History*, 17, no. 4 (1976): 488–89.

50. William Derman, *Serfs, Peasants, and Socialists: A Former Serf Village in the Republic of Guinea* (Berkeley, California: University of California Press, 1973), p. 30.

51. Derman, *Serfs, Peasants, and Socialists*, p. 34.

52. Frederick Cooper, *Plantation Slavery on the East Coast of Africa* (New Haven: Yale University Press, 1977), pp. xi, 156–70.

53. Cooper, *Plantation Slavery*, p. 173.

54. Cooper, *Plantation Slavery*, p. 173–76, 228.

55. Cooper, *Plantation Slavery*, pp. 51, 52, 61, 131, 221–25.

56. Klein, "The Study of Slavery," p. 605.

57. Allen Isaacman and Anton Rosenthal, "Slaves, Soldiers, and Police: Power and Dependency among the Chikunda of Mozambique, ca. 1825–1920," in *The End of Slavery*, pp. 220–53.

58. Walter Rodney, "African Slavery and Other Forms of Social Oppression on the Upper Guinea Coast in the Context of the Atlantic Slave Trade," *Journal of African History*, 7, no. 3 (1966): 431–43; John D. Fage, "Slaves and Society in Western Africa, c. 1445–1700," *Journal of African History*, 21 (1980): 289–310; Claude Meillassoux, "The Role of Slavery in the Economic and Social History of Sahelo-Sudanic Africa," in *Forced Migration: The Impact of the Export Slave Trade on African Societies*, edited by Joseph E. Inikori (London and New York: Hutchinson and Africana, 1982), pp. 74–99; J. Devisse and S. Labib, "Africa in Inter-Continental Relations," in *UNESCO General History of Africa: IV, Africa from the Twelfth to the Sixteenth Century*, edited by D. T. Niane (Berkeley: Heinemann, University of California Press, UNESCO, 1984), p. 672.

59. S. M. Cissoko, "The Songhay from the 12th to the 16th Century," in *UNESCO General History*, pp. 202–203.

60. Cissoko, "The Songhay," p. 205.

61. Niane, *UNESCO General History*, p. 682.

62. Ivor Wilks, "Land, Labour, Capital and the Forest Kingdom of Asante: A Model of Early Change," in *The Evolution of Social Systems*, edited by J. Friedman and M. J. Rowlands (London: Duckworth, 1977), pp. 523–24.

63. Anne Hilton, *The Kingdom of Kongo* (Oxford: Clarendon, 1985), pp. 32–35.

64. Hilton, *Kingdom of Kongo*, p. 233, n. 86.

65. Jan Vansina, *Paths in the Rainforests: Toward a History of Political Tradition in Equatorial Africa* (London: James Currey, 1990), p. 278; Vansina, "Deep-Down Time: Political Tradition in Central Africa," *History*

in Africa, 16 (1989): 352. The latter work shows the spread of the term from the slave trading coastal communities to the interior, along the main trade routes (p. 353, map 3).

66. John Thornton, *Africa and Africans in the Making of the Atlantic World, 1400–1680* (Cambridge: Cambridge University Press, 1992), p. 74. This book focuses on a very important subject — the contribution of Africa and Africans to the history of the Atlantic basin; unfortunately, it is marred by conceptual weakness and factual inaccuracies. For example, the statement that "The average density in seventeenth-century Lower Guinea . . . was probably well over thirty people per square kilometer, or well over the average European density of the time" (p. 75) has no empirical foundation, both on the European and on the African side. The population of Western Europe was 61 million in 1200, 73 million in 1300, and 78 million in 1550 (D. C. North and R. P. Thomas, *The Rise of the Western World* [Cambridge: Cambridge University Press, 1971], p. 71). With a land area of 898,804 square miles, the average densities come to 68 persons per square mile in 1200, 81 in 1300, and 87 in 1550. Average densities in Western Africa did not reach these levels until the colonial period. It was these relatively high population densities of Western Europe, and the growth of trade and the commercialization of socio-economic life to which they gave rise, that provoked the development of private property rights in land in Western Europe. The economics and the empirical basis of Thornton's arguments are, therefore, dubious.

67. Douglass C. North and Robert P. Thomas, *The Rise of the Western World: A New Economic History* (Cambridge: Cambridge University Press, 1973), p. 63.

68. Goody, "Feudalism in Africa?," p. 6.

69. North and Thomas, *The Rise of the Western World*, p. 88.

70. Hilton, *Kingdom of Kongo*, p. 57.

71. Hilton, *Kingdom of Kongo*, p. 78.

72. Hilton, *Kingdom of Kongo*, pp. 58, 78, 85, 122–23; see also John K. Thornton, *The Kingdom of Kongo: Civil War and Transition, 1641–1718* (Madison: University of Wisconsin Press, 1983), pp. 15–27, which describes the urban setting for slave employment but does not trace the historical development of slavery in Kongo. Research in other regions shows a similar pattern. See Robert W. Harms, *River of Wealth, River of Sorrow: The Central Zaire Basin in the Era of the Slave and Ivory Trade, 1500–1891* (New Haven: Yale University Press, 1981); Ralph Austen, "Slavery among Coastal Middlemen: The Duala of Cameroon," in *Slavery in Africa;* Joseph E. Inikori, *The Chaining of a Continent: Export Demand for Captives and the History of Africa South of the Sahara, 1450–1870* (Mona, Jamaica: Institute of Social and Economic Research, 1992), pp.

25–39; Patrick Manning, *Slavery and African Life: Occidental, Oriental, and African Slave Trades* (Cambridge: Cambridge University Press, 1990); and Meillassoux, *The Anthropology of Slavery*, pp. 33, 40, 43, 70, 239–40.

73. Rodney, "African Slavery and Other Forms of Social Oppression," pp. 431–33.
74. Klein, "The Study of Slavery," p. 605.
75. Paul E. Lovejoy, *Transformations in Slavery: A History of Slavery in Africa* (Cambridge: Cambridge University Press, 1983).

Rethinking
American Slavery

COLIN A. PALMER

Over two decades ago when I decided to do a dissertation on slavery, one of my graduate-student peers questioned my choice on the grounds that it was a "dead" subject. Although my focus was to be on Mexico, my colleague believed that, despite their interpretive differences, Stanley Elkins and Kenneth Stampp had said the last words on that historical problem and there was no need for any additional research. I ignored the advice, conducted the research, and later I was asked to make a contribution to an edited work on slavery and race relations. My contribution — and this was around 1970 — argued that the enslaved whom I studied had been able to create and maintain a culture that was uniquely theirs. I shall always remember — and treasure — the reaction of the person who read the manuscript for the press: undoubtedly influenced by the prevailing scholarship and the notion that slaves became "Sambos," the reader declared, "This person has no mature understanding of slavery." Angry and humiliated, I tore up the comment and withdrew the piece. Of course, this was before John Blassingame, Charles Joyner, George Rawick, Herbert Gutman, Eugene Genovese, Franklin Knight, and a host of other scholars enlarged our understanding of the cultures created by the enslaved and their struggles to leave their imprint on the land they shared with others. In fact, a few of these studies have painted such an idyllic picture of slave life, in contrast to that depicted by Elkins and Stampp, that the time has come for another look, a reassessment of the experiences of America's enslaved population.[1]

Writing about slavery studies in the late 1970s, David Hackett Fischer observed that "history is now being shaken to its very foundation by an intellectual revolution which may in time prove to be more profound in its effects than the discovery of quantum physics, or the invention of evolutionary biology, or the developments of classical archeology."[2] Those of us who are engaged in such studies would agree that methodological advances and several exciting new conclusions constitute a veritable intellectual revolution. Not only have historians asked different and more sophisticated questions of the traditional records, but new documentary sources, chiefly those left by those who were enslaved, have been exploited. The earlier notion that slave narratives and autobiographies could not be relied upon to provide an informed and credible picture of slave life has given way to innovative uses of these rich and remarkable sources. Historians of slavery finally took note of Richard Hofstadter's 1944 charge that "any history of slavery must be written in large measure from the standpoint of the slave."[3]

Recently scholars have produced sensitive portraits of slave life, and we now have a fuller picture of how these persons ordered their lives, the institutions they created, the exuberant cultures they produced, and their efforts to transform their condition. The image of the broken, traumatized Sambo has been replaced in some renderings with that of the resilient, Teflon-coated person who endured much but also created much, and who walked away from his or her oppression — at least those who were around after Emancipation — relatively unscathed psychologically.

While these new conclusions have much to recommend them, I fear that several historians, particularly American historians, now run the risk of presenting a picture of slavery that is just as distorted as the ones they seek to correct. In responding to Elkins's thesis, they have in some instances come dangerously close to sanitizing slavery of its terror, its inhumanity, and its unspeakable denial of basic human rights. In fact, we cannot fully comprehend the meaning of slavery for the enslaved unless we have a deep understanding of the power relationships that undergirded the institution and the terrible ways in which the lives of those considered property were circumscribed, blighted, and destroyed.

African slavery was introduced into Hispaniola in 1502, more than

one hundred years before those "twenty and odd" black persons dis-
embarked from that Dutch ship at Jamestown in 1619. This fact is not
normally considered by American historians who wrestle with such
questions as the origins of racial slavery in North America. The answer
to the important question of origins cannot be sought without an ap-
preciation of the ways in which Africans were treated in Europe, particularly in Spain and Portugal, prior to their arrival in Hispaniola. We are
now beginning to understand that by the fifteenth century, the Spaniards, the Portuguese, and probably other Europeans had already assumed a posture of superiority over black Africans, based on cultural or
phenotypical (racial) differences. This posture was not simply a prejudice directed against the "Other"; some scholars are now suggesting
that by the end of the European Middle Ages the terms *slavery* and *race*
were becoming interchangeable and negative "racial" characteristics began to be applied to Africans in intellectual and public discourse.[4] By
the mid-nineteenth century a virulent racist ideology had emerged in
some societies of the Americas to give legitimacy to the mistreatment
of the peoples of African descent, but this assertion of white supremacy
was only new in the sense that its claims rested increasingly on pseudo-
scientific data. Such data gave theoretical respectability to what had long
existed in practice.

Centuries before they colonized the Americas, Europeans had embraced the concept of property in persons. Slavery existed throughout
Christendom, and Muslims, Slavs, Turks, and Africans formed the bulk
of the servile populations. While some of the enslaved were natives of
the society that enslaved them, the majority were outsiders. The fact
that slavery tended to be primarily exogenous in Europe was not in itself
unusual. But it is significant that the enslaved were the quintessential
"Other," the persons set apart from other members of the society by
virtue of their religion, phenotype, broad cultural attributes, or conquered status.

No society that owned slaves was blind to the differences separating
the dominant group from the enslaved. The fundamental question, to
be sure, was the meaning that the various controlling elites placed on
these differences and whether they were deemed immutable. The Christian elites knew that Jews, if they so desired, could change the religious
beliefs and practices that helped account for their oppression. In the case
of endogenous slavery, some elites knew that those among the enslaved
who shared their culture and phenotype could make the appropriate
transition to freedom.

The situation is much more murky where both phenotypical and cultural chasms separated masters from their slaves. Among peoples famous for their ethnocentric judgments, it would be surprising if these differences were respected, much less celebrated. Under the circumstances, the acquisition of black African slaves — particularly by the Spaniards, the Portuguese, the French, and the Italians during the late Middle Ages — must have elicited varying responses and judgments. When the first large group of Africans arrived in Lisbon in 1444, the chronicler, Gomes Eanes de Zurara, reported that the captives "were a marvelous sight; for amongst them were some white enough, fair to look upon and well proportioned; others were less white like mulattoes; others again were as black as Ethiops and so ugly, both in features and in body, as almost to appear (to those who saw them) the images of a lower hemisphere . . . some kept their heads low and their faces bathed in tears."[5]

The historian of the early black presence in Portugal, A. C. De C. M. Saunders, concludes that "most Portuguese seem to have thought that blacks as a people were innately inferior to whites in physical beauty and mental ability and, moreover, that they were temperamentally suited to a life of slavery."[6] The color black "signified misfortune and sadness." Furthermore, "it was held to be the skin colour of the devils in hell."[7] Contemporary Portuguese literature depicted blacks as dim-witted, loyal, good humored, and generally contented with their enslaved condition. The Africans' condition was deemed to be a function of divine punishment, a result of the curse of Ham. In fact, Zurara was also convinced of the innate suitability of West Africans for slavery because they were "living so like beasts, with no law of reasonable creatures; nor did they know what bread, wine, clothing or houses were; and what was worse, because of their great ignorance they had no knowledge of good, only of living in bestial sloth."[8] Slavery rescued such Africans, provided them with the benefits of Christianity and introduced them to the transforming influences of European culture.

As in the case of Portugal, there are indications that during the fifteenth century most slaves in Spain were of African descent. They had for the most part replaced Muslim prisoners of war, who had hitherto constituted the majority of the slave population. Andalusian towns, particularly Seville, were the homes of the largest number of Africans. In 1479 the Spaniards signed the Treaty of Alcáçovas with the Portuguese, granting traders in that country the right to supply Spaniards with enslaved Africans. Ruth Pike also notes that by "the reign of Ferdinand and Isabella, the Negro population of Seville had grown so large that the Catholic Kings decided to place them under greater royal supervision and control."[9]

As outsiders and as slaves, Africans existed on the periphery of Spanish society. Pike found that in Seville the "whites showed their contempt for Negroes with the customary sidewalk jeer (estornudo)"[10] As the Africans hailed from different cultural and religious backgrounds, the Spaniards attempted to hispanicize as well as christianize them — an early assumption of the white man's burden. Buttressing this desire to change the African culturally was a pervasive belief in the superior ways of the dominant society.

Recent research shows that by the fifteenth century Europeans had developed various criteria for classifying persons, including physical and behavioral characteristics. The concept of the inherent superiority of some individuals and the natural inferiority of others had long been familiar to the literate public through the works of Aristotle, and the work of the Aristotelian scholar Juan Ginés de Sepúlveda demonstrates that the doctrine of natural slavery was alive and well in Spain in the mid-sixteenth century. In justifying the subjugation of the indigenous peoples of the Americas, Sepúlveda asserted:

> The man rules over the woman, the adult over the child, the father over his children. That is to say, the most powerful and the most perfect rule over the weakest and most imperfect. The same relationship exists among men, there being some who by nature are masters and others who by nature are slaves. Those who surpass the rest in prudence and intelligence, although not in physical strength, are by nature the masters. On the other hand, those who are dim-witted and mentally lazy, although they may be physically strong enough to fulfill all the necessary tasks, are by nature, slaves. It is just and useful that it be this way."[11]

Aristotle's theory of natural slavery and Sepúlveda's interpretation of it predate the modern concept upon which racist ideology is based. Some years before Sepúlveda, Dante had extended Aristotle's arguments to include entire races, thereby granting legitimacy to Rome's territorial aggrandizement. We cannot claim that the ideas of Aristotle or Dante constituted parts of the popular discourse in Spain or Portugal — or elsewhere, for that matter — in the years preceding the colonization of the Americas. Like all other peoples, however, the citizens of these countries would have been attuned to the values and beliefs that gave their societies life. In these hierarchical societies, the dominant ideology explained and legitimized inequality and the existing varieties of oppression.

But such ideologies were always elastic in their expression and in their ability to explain new or old forms of exploitation. While slavery was justified in the Middle Ages on such grounds as conquest, religious differences, and moral defect, nineteenth century apologists, themselves the product of a secular and scientific age, called upon the fruits of "scientific" research in defense of property in black persons. In this sense, the current preoccupation with making a neat distinction between a modern "scientific" racism and the prejudice of earlier times is not always illuminating.[12] The Western world of the Enlightenment looked to science to explain and legitimize certain forms of political and social behavior; an earlier world had different explanations and justifications.

In the case of the Africans in Europe, particularly in the Iberian peninsula, there is ample evidence to indicate that white attitudes toward them did not harden overnight, probably because black Africans were never present in significant numbers anywhere until the fifteenth century. Surviving records suggest that the early European perceptions of these strangers were neither uniformly positive nor negative. The European mind seemed to have constructed at one extreme an image of Africa as a land of monsters, and at the other, a land of wealth and abundance as reflected in the legend of Prester John that celebrated the existence of a powerful kingdom somewhere on the continent. These and other constructed images existed simultaneously but they were never fixed, either in terms of their content or the intensity with which they were embraced.

By the time Columbus crossed the Atlantic, however, African slavery had become commonplace on the Iberian peninsula and the image of Africa had been shorn of any positive characteristics. Sylvia Wynter notes that even the image of Prester John "fades".[13] Ronald Sanders also observes that the image of this noble Ethiopian had become vulnerable "in an era when Christian fanaticism against the Jew came together with a loathing for the waves of black captives that began rolling off those very Portuguese ships that had gone searching for Prester John in the first place."[14]

Although the subordination of the black outsider had become complete by the late fifteenth century, Iberians had not yet developed a coherent secular ideology to explain and legitimize the assumed superiority of one group and the assumed inferiority of the other. Perhaps none was necessary or needed in a prescientific age where the "Other" could be easily dismissed as a barbarian and devalued. According to

Anthony Pagden, the word *barbaros* "had become, and was forever to remain, a word which was used only of cultural or mental inferiors." He notes that the only thing all the usages of the word shared "was the implication of inferiority."[15]

The Spanish colonists brought to the Americas, then, not only a familiarity with property in persons, but also a mental conditioning that assumed their superiority over other peoples, particularly "barbarians." Their zeitgeist did not celebrate human differences, nor did it accord all races and their modes of behavior equal value. It is this zeitgeist that helps explain the reduction of the indigenous peoples of the Americas to a condition of servitude, as well as the concurrent enslavement of African peoples.

From the outset of the invasion, Christopher Columbus and his men never appear to have envisaged a relationship with the indigenous peoples other than that of the superior and the subordinate. The residents of the Caribbean islands were not engaged in a war with the Spaniards, so it cannot be maintained that they suffered the traditional fate of conquered peoples by losing their liberty and their land. The planting of the Spanish flag on these islands and the imposition of colonial rule defined the nature of the relationship from the moment of contact. The assertion of Spanish authority was not made gradually; it was immediate and supported by the developing might of the colonial state.

When the indigenous peoples of the Caribbean began to experience a demographic decline, the Spaniards attempted to locate an alternative source of exploited labor. There were several options open to them. In the first place, the colonists could have abandoned the colonial enterprise and returned home. This possibility was evidently not considered. Second, they could have relied on their own energies to exploit the resources of the colonies that they had established. Generations of historians have emphasized that many of the Spaniards who came to the Americas disdained manual labor, thereby unwittingly lending a curious aura of legitimacy to the use of indigenous or imported slave labor. But the fact remains that some Spaniards did perform their own labor services, so manual labor and a Spanish background were not incompatible.

It is also conceivable that Spaniards could have introduced a system of indentured labor, as the English would do a century later. We can find no evidence that this was discussed. In any event, there was nothing inevitable about the introduction and use of African slave labor. There was no irresistible magic wand that compelled the Spaniards to replace exploited native workers with black slaves. It was a voluntary and conscious decision rooted in past practice and in a social zeitgeist that legitimized property in persons and one that had increasingly come to associate such a condition with the black "Other." When the indigenous peoples succumbed, the Spaniards turned to the Africans, who were slaves in the world that they had left.

It is instructive that early records do not reveal any debate over the introduction of Africans into the Americas as slaves. Perhaps, as the preceding argument suggests, there was a presumption of the normalcy of such a condition for Africans. Consequently, when the governor of Hispaniola, Nicolás de Ovando, made his request to the Crown for African slaves in 1501, he needed to justify it solely in terms of the need for labor. The Crown's acquiescence was not unusual, since African slavery had become commonplace in Spain.

The first cargo of hispanicized African slaves arrived in Hispaniola in 1502, inaugurating almost four centuries of black slavery in the Americas. In accordance with the economic needs of the colonists, the institution of slavery would soon spread to Cuba, Puerto Rico, Jamaica, and the mainland. Unlike the Europeans, these Africans did not make a conscious decision to seek their fortunes in a new land; they came as property. It is important to underscore the point because this fact has shaped the nature of black life in this hemisphere and the texture of the relationships between the races.

The black slave population experienced a steady expansion in Spain's empire throughout the sixteenth century. In 1516 the Dominican friar, Bartolomé de las Casas, urged the importation of black labor to replace the Indians who were dying because of overwork and mistreatment by the Spaniards. A year later, the Hieronymite friars urged that *bozales,* or Africans unacculturated to Spanish ways, be sent to Hispaniola and Puerto Rico to alleviate the acute labor shortage. Other voices joined in making such an appeal. Charles V was persuaded by these petitions and allowed the direct importation of slaves from Africa in 1518.

Our concern here is not with the details of the slave trade. Rather, we stress the point that these requests seemed to rest on the premise that Africans and their labor were there for the asking. The coldly dispassionate tone of the requests is similar to any that would have been made for tools, seeds, or textiles. Africans had become the dehumanized and servile hewers of wood and drawers of water. Equally noticeable is the fact that the church joined the colonists and the political authorities in endorsing African slave labor. Thus, the three principal groups of colonists agreed not only on the necessity for slave labor, but also on what peoples should be consigned to that fate. There was no such unanimity in the case of the indigenous peoples, although there was considerable support for their enslavement.

The claim is not being made here that the Spaniards used a double standard in their relationships with the indigenous peoples and the Africans. The matter is not so simple. In fact, it can be argued that the response of the Spaniards to the peoples of the Caribbean islands, on the one hand, and to the Aztec and the Inca, on the other, was significantly different. The achievements of the indigenous peoples in the mainland empires impressed the invaders in a way the island societies never did. Although the Spaniards succeeded in establishing political control over all of these peoples, they could not lightly dismiss the sophisticated highland civilizations of the Incas and the Aztecs, and they had to confront questions relating to the legitimacy of their rule and the justice of the conquest. Friar Antonio de Montesinos had denounced the mistreatment of the peoples of Hispaniola in 1511, but it was not until after the defeat of the more materially advanced Aztecs and Incas that the rights of the conquered peoples became a subject of sustained discussion. In 1539, for example, the Dominican jurist Francisco de Vitoria delivered a series of lectures at the University of Salamanca questioning the legitimacy of Spain's colonization of the Americas. Now recognized as one of the earliest proponents of the study of international law, Vitoria rejected the crown's claim to exercise jurisdiction over other peoples, particularly if they did not oppose Christianity, practice cannibalism, or prevent the Spaniards from peacefully residing among them and conducting trade.[16]

There were no immediate answers to the concerns raised by Vitoria and other critics. The colonial experience was a new one for the Spaniards, thus they lacked a precedent for both policy and behavior. Complicating the problem was the fact that the colonized were recognized as Spanish subjects, presumably entitled to all of the customary protection and rights that flowed therefrom. There were also, not surprisingly, considerable doubts as to whether the indigenous peoples, in spite of their respected achievements, could claim equal membership in the human family.

For our purposes, the central point is that the question of the legitimate place of Africans in Spanish society, in contrast to that of the Indians, was resolved *prior* to the colonial enterprise. There can be no doubt that the enslavement of such persons had come to be seen as legally justifiable and morally acceptable. We have no evidence to suggest that this was ever an anguished decision, the subject of any discourse among members of the literate public.

The African was, of course, an outsider in both Spain and in the Americas, defined and treated as such. His was a purchased body, with all of its awful consequences. Some apologists argued that his enslavement was an improvement over his prior condition; even Francisco de Vitoria could claim that, provided the Africans "are treated humanly, it is better for them to be slaves among Christians than free in their own lands."[17] Few Spaniards at the time would have disagreed with this conclusion. Referring to the slave trade, one contemporary jurist nonchalantly maintained, "It is not necessary for us to examine whether the captivity of a Negro is just or not, because the sale is presumed to be just unless there is evidence of injustice."[18] Our reading of this comment suggests that the issue was not the legitimacy of slavery, but rather the process by which slaves were acquired. Not until centuries later would the morality of the institution be questioned in Europe and the Americas. Ironically, however, the abolitionist movement and the proponents of pseudo-scientific racism emerged almost simultaneously.

The debasement of the Africans as slaves, and as human beings, was a process that had its antecedents in Europe. David Brion Davis maintains that "from the start, the Moors and Negroes . . . formed the lowest rank of slaves."[19] Noting the influence of the Muslims, William McKee Evans has argued that by the late Middle Ages:

> not only did slavery become largely a racial institution in a broad core of countries extending from Andalusia to the Indian Ocean, but a related development also took place in these countries that forged even tighter links between blackness and debasement, links that have endured into the modern era. As early as the ninth century, racial stratification began to appear both in the servile and the free populations.[20]

Anthony Padgen has also speculated that the Spaniards perceived white slaves from the Balkans and the Black Sea differently from other slaves, and that they may have enjoyed "a higher measure of respect within the family than either the Africans or the Indians were to do."[21] Clearly, the negative perceptions of blacks shared by Europeans did not originate in the Americas, nor did they begin with the momentous events of 1492.

Racial slavery found its greatest ideological expression in North America. Why this occurred is properly the subject of another analysis. Suffice it to say, when the first Africans were purchased in Jamestown in 1619, blacks had been commodities of trade in the Americas for over a century and their place in the societies of the Spanish and the Portuguese had been well established.[22] The English adopted the institution, but like the other Europeans before them, they had to create — slowly but surely—a zeitgeist that sanctioned property in black persons. This emerged over time and had assumed, for a variety of reasons, a distinctive racist bellicosity by the nineteenth century. But we must not conclude that the North American racial trajectory was exceptional or sui generis. Its roots were planted elsewhere, at an earlier time. What was new about the societies of the Americas was that racism became deeply embedded in the societal core; it became systemic. It is this development that largely explains its longevity.

I have dealt at some length with the European antecedents of racial slavery precisely because we should no longer discuss the history of the enslavement of African peoples in one society in complete isolation from its trajectory in others. Historians of the African diaspora have increasingly come to recognize that the texture of slavery in the Americas and in Europe manifested broad similarities, although it depended on local and material circumstances as well. Similarly, the ideology that legitimized racial slavery knew no societal boundaries, although the timing, content, and virulence of its expression varied. Racial slavery in North America drew upon the experiences of other peoples, even as it developed its own characteristics.

Exploring the roots of racial slavery and racial ideology, however, is not synonymous with studying the institution of slavery and the interior lives of the enslaved. Consequently, much of the recent scholarship has been driven by the need to tell the slaves' story essentially from their perspective. Still, one of the weaknesses of the current historiography as it relates to blacks is the failure to transform the existing paradigms derived or borrowed from the study of the history of the larger society. The watersheds that have defined the history of whites and others, for example, have been applied arbitrarily to the history of blacks. But the history of any people must reflect their own experiences, must possess its own internal markers or watersheds.

Prior to 1865, the internal markers for blacks appear to be the 1730s and the 1820s; times that ushered in or at least reflected significant new departures in the trajectory of the peoples of African descent. The demographic studies of Russell Menard, Peter Wood, Alan Kulikoff, and others have shown that by the 1730s a creole or local-born population had begun to emerge.[23] There was an annual rate of natural increase, a process that brought what I have called "the long first century" (1619–1730) to an end. This emerging creole population would, in time, become the dominant group, spanning African and American worlds and drawing its strength, inspiration, and culture from both. Hitherto, the flavor of black life in America had been primarily African in all of its richness, complexity, and diversity. With the appearance of a significant number of persons who were born and socialized into the customs of a new land and subjected to their transforming influences, the texture of their lives and world views was altered. This demographic change had profound consequences for the development and shaping of a black culture, consciousness, and identity.

The first two decades of the nineteenth century represented a second watershed in the historical trajectory of black America. By 1820 the inner fabric of black life had become well defined in a multitude of ways. In fact, by the early 1800s most of the enslaved were creoles, suggesting a profound demographic and even structural change; many had become Christians of a sort and spoke English, and a black community characterized by similar core understandings had begun to assume its distinctive shape.

The period 1820–65 saw the crystallization of a slave community—a development that was, in large measure, a consequence of the end of the slave trade and the emergence of the creoles as the dominant group in slave society. The forty-five years spanning the period witnessed a 150 percent increase in the slave population, reflecting an average annual increase of 2.4 percent. These years saw the appearance of a highly talented group of free black leaders, physical challenges to the institution of slavery, the proliferation of black institutions, the rise of the abolitionist movement, and so on.

Thus, between 1619 and 1865 we can identify two important watersheds in black life, each representing a significant point of departure and driven by internal forces. When viewing this history from the perspective of blacks, therefore, we cannot follow traditional markers such as the colonial period, the revolutionary period, or the antebellum period. While important for understanding the evolution of the larger society, they tell us little about the real stuff of an internal black history—its woof and warp. These observations are also applicable to the various slave societies of the Caribbean and Latin America.

But what about the study of slavery itself, the prevailing interpretive currents and the need for reassessment? Without dwelling on all of the developments of the last two decades, suffice it to note that a significant proportion of the scholarship, particularly that treating North America, has presented a picture of slavery that is static and sugarcoated. Much of this literature focuses on the nineteenth century, particularly the period 1820–60, the period in which slavery reached its apogee and which affords the richest and most accessible documentation.

Although there is a tendency to frame generalizations about slavery based upon the experiences of these four decades, it must be recalled that the institution lasted for two-and-a-half centuries. The picture that emerges in most of the literature is characterized by stasis and a distressing homogenizing of slave life. Many of these works pay insufficient attention to the changing demographic structure of the slave population, the variegated nature of their work routines, or even whether the group being discussed was composed primarily of African-born persons (as was the case in the seventeenth and for much of the eighteenth centuries) or of creoles. Even our best historians tend to ignore the differences between the life trajectories and cultural moorings of the African-born and the creole slaves.

Similarly, almost all of our slavery scholars show an abysmal ignorance of African history: the nature of the societies from which the enslaved Africans came, their world views, their cultural assumptions, and so on. The result has been a series of studies that do not situate the African-born in their cultures, but impose Western paradigms and constructs on peoples whose zeitgeist and social arrangements were fundamentally dissimilar. The slave trade was more than a movement of peoples. Africa, in all of its cultural richness and diversity, came to the Americas, as well, and African cultural sensibilities informed much of black life in the quarters and beyond.

I am not suggesting that African cultural institutions were transported to America, where they were reproduced in a mechanistic fashion. Instead, I would contend that Africa came to the Americas with the enslaved and that a deep understanding of African societies will help us appreciate the family arrangements, religious beliefs, gender relationships, child-rearing practices, and the nature of resistance, among other issues, in the quarters.

In fact, it is precisely because many of our scholars are not deeply schooled in African history that some of their work on slavery in the Americas is flawed. In addition, some scholars have kept too close an eye on the pulse of the contemporary public, distorting the history of the black past to satisfy current imperatives. There is also an acute methodological fuzziness surrounding the related but essentially different questions regarding the impact of slavery on its victims, on the one hand, and the degree to which slaves were able to create and sustain vibrant cultures, on the other. Although scholars now uniformly celebrate the cultural achievements of the enslaved, particularly in the nineteenth century, they are reluctant to address the troubling but crucial question of the ways in which the institution affected and blighted the human possibilities of its victims.

To grant the possibility that slavery must have had a deleterious impact on its victims is fundamentally to affirm the humanity of the black person.[24] No one needs to make patronizing and unrealistic claims about the psychic strength of people of African descent. Africans and their children were people, too, with all of the vulnerabilities and strengths manifested by humans everywhere. Their pain and burdens in the Americas were great and unremitting, and their struggles to maintain their selfhood were extraordinary. But in the end these sustained struggles must have exacted a toll, and everyone must have paid a psychic price. Slavery was no picnic, and those who experienced it never claimed it to be so.

To be sure, the culture of slaves everywhere in the Americas helped provide them with the basis of their psychological sustenance. Their culture both defined and shaped them. It was constantly changing in accordance with new realities, although there were many continuities, as well. But this culture lacked the absolute power, the independent agency that some scholars have ascribed to it to neutralize and render ineffective racial slavery's cannons. The slaves' culture and their networks of relationships tempered the effects of the psychic wounds that were inflicted, but they could not prevent the targets from being hit from a multitude of directions. Nor could this culture and its support systems always kill the pain, heal the wounds, or remove the scars.

How the institution of slavery affected the personhood of its victims will probably never be fully understood. It can be argued, however, that there was a wide range of psychological responses to the institution. These responses must have been shaped by a number of variables, such as whether the person was African or American born; the age at which an African was enslaved in the Americas; the size of the black population at any one time; the presence or absence of cultural institutions; and the degree, frequency, and nature of interaction with whites. Generalizations that seek to create simple categories of personality types for slaves are flawed at best. They are not time-specific; they fail to recognize the variegated nature of the slaves' experiences; and they often use analytical models that have no bearing on the unique experiences of black slaves exposed to systemic debasement for over two centuries by whites in a white-dominated society.

The psychic price that these people paid as the victims of oppression must have been great. Yet, although no one could escape slavery's pernicious reach and unholy influence, not everyone was affected in the same way. Some must have become the traumatized, broken, psychologically maimed Sambo that white Southerners described during the nineteenth century. At the other extreme, sheer mental fortitude and luck helped others avoid most of the damaging influences of the institution that held them in thrall. In between — and constituting the vast majority — were a range of personality types: persons who, in varying degrees, bore psychic scars as a consequence of their condition, but who were neither so traumatized as to become Sambos nor possessors of Teflon-coated personalities. Like most persons today, they functioned normally in spite of their travail, took their blows in stride, and proceeded to confront the next challenge. Most slaves maintained a psychic balance, but no one was immune to the psychic pain that slavery brought.

We also need a much more nuanced interpretation of the important and controversial question of resistance. This is probably the most glamorous issue for recent historians, and in some renderings every act by the enslaved is deemed politically motivated and inspired. Such may have been the case in some situations, but we must grant that not every act by a slave was dictated by whites or constituted a conscious reaction to their power. Slaves were often independent actors, the enormous reach of whites notwithstanding.

To be sure, slaves did engage in a variety of forms of resistance: from flight to rebellions to malingering. John Blassingame has recently suggested that nine rebellions (in contrast to "conspiracies") occurred between 1619 and 1860. A resort to organized violence was, however, not an everyday occurrence. Slaves were not always on the barricades; most had to confront daily and more mundane struggles for survival. But there are some very compelling reasons, I believe, why the enslaved never posed a successful violent challenge to slavery. During the long first century, Africans and their children constituted a small minority of the overall population of the colonies and were distributed over a vast geographic area. With their lives disrupted and lacking a critical mass of their peers, Africans offered only one violent and notable challenge to slavery before 1720. The New York rebellion of 1712 took place in an urban area that had a slave population of slightly less than one thousand — a seemingly inadequate number to take on the armed might of the whites, even if there had been full participation.

I am inclined to believe that there may have been cultural imperatives at work among the African-born that discouraged the use of violence in some situations. The nature of the slaves' resistance, as with other aspects of their behavior, had to be culturally sanctioned. As Monica Schuler and others have shown, some Africans perceived slavery as a misfortune and the consequence of sorcery.[25] Such sorcery could be defeated not by a resort to violence but by the successful application of a stronger and superior form of sorcery by the victims. Thus, some members of a deeply religious enslaved population contested the power of their enslavers by drawing upon their arsenal of religious beliefs and practices. That this was largely ineffective in a Western environment is beside the point. In time, a larger and more creolized slave population, at least in North America, would show a greater tendency to conspire and embrace violence to end their oppression.

Yet there was never a rebellion anywhere in North America that involved the participation of more than a few hundred slaves. In addition, a resort to organized violence was not a particularly frequent occurrence even by creoles in the nineteenth century. There are several factors that may help us understand why this was the case. We cannot ignore the fact that white society had a monopoly of armed power, watched the servile population very closely, and punished threats to the social order swiftly and brutally. The controlling mechanisms of white society—the army, militia, local patrols, and the judiciary—bolstered the enormous private disciplinary power that slave owners or their surrogates wielded. White society's self-proclaimed racial superiority over the peoples of African descent—slave or free—legitimized its exercise of power. Ironically, however, it also led an insecure white society to remain frenetically vigilant, fearful of threats to the social order and devoting much energy to its protection. Slaves, in retrospect, stood little chance of success if they openly assaulted such a system; the forces arrayed against them were too powerful and deeply entrenched.

There were other limiting factors, as well. In terms of its size, the slave population of the nineteenth century posed the greatest potential challenge to the institution. But it was a population constantly beset by externally induced problems that consumed much of its psychic energies. The appalling, forcible break-up of an estimated two million marriages between 1820 and 1860 and the massive removal of probably as many as one million persons from the Upper South to the Lower South after 1790 created untold misery in black lives. Starkly reminiscent of the disruptions caused by the international slave trade, such atrocities contradict the uniform picture of a sedentary slave population in the nineteenth century.

Under different circumstances, such unremitting pressures probably would have produced more frequent organized violent responses. But slaves, it seems, were acutely aware of the impossibility of defeating the whites, given the absence of military wherewithal. They were, however, able to take advantage of divisions in white society to claim their freedom—first during the war for American independence, and then, when white America went to war with itself in 1861, many thousands of the enslaved also seized the opportunity to liberate themselves.

The insecurity of their lives and the disruptions notwithstanding, slaves had to function as people. The spectacular population growth after 1820 — in spite of a high infant mortality rate — tells us much about the world of the slaves and its inner drives. Fully seventy-three percent of the slaves were under age thirty in 1860; a high proportion of them were children. Family ties, concern for the safety of kith and kin, and the presence of a disproportionate number of children not likely to have yet experienced slavery in all of its horror were all factors that must have blunted any tendency towards violent resistance. If slavery's end had not been hastened by the Civil War, a large, mature, and numerically confi-dent slave population would have eventually fulfilled white society's worst nightmare.

White society's arsenal of control was not limited to the exercise of physical power. We know that the larger society attempted to debase blacks and to inflict countless psychological wounds on them. Although the majority of the black population succeeded in maintaining a psychic balance, we cannot fully comprehend the nature of the internal price they paid. The struggle to maintain a degree of selfhood and to reject or at least place limits on the hegemonic power of whites remains the most poignant and compelling aspect of the black odyssey. The most sustained struggle against slavery took place in the heads of its victims, in their battle against becoming psychological lepers or the compliant robots that their masters desired.

Enslaved peoples struggled to meet their own needs as individuals, lovers, parents, children, and friends. These quiet battles were not spec-tacular, nor were they unusual, but these human challenges were infi-nitely more difficult for the enslaved to confront than they were for those who owned them, and more debilitating in their demands. Such overt acts of resistance as flight and rebellion elicited a kind of courage that many did not have. Yet those who worked to meet their own needs, as well as those of kith and kin, carving passageways in slavery's complex edifice also demonstrated compelling resilience, courage, and inner strength. Resistance was more than just an act of violence or escape; for the slave population it was a relentless struggle to maintain their humanity.

Historians have also not avoided methodological pitfalls in their analyses of such important aspects of slaves' lives as their family arrange-ments, religious beliefs, and practices. Any analysis of the kin arrange-ments and the family life of the African-born slaves (and to some extent that of the creoles) must be approached with caution: we must be careful not to invoke Western conceptualizations and seek to identify only examples of Christian marriages, monogamy, and the standard nuclear family. Africans enjoyed kin and familial traditions quite different from those of Christian Europeans, and it is unfortunate that some historians and others have applied Western models of kinship arrangements, such as the nuclear family, simple family, extended family, etc., to peoples who did not organize themselves in such a way. The result is that we have used a measure of their kin arrangements that lacks cultural validity. It is only when the black population becomes creolized and to some extent Christianized that we can begin to apply, albeit cautiously, Western concepts in this area. Accordingly, kinship arrangements must not be viewed simply as an extension of or a carbon copy of those of the whites. To do so is to seriously misunderstand the evolution of black life and the ideas that informed and legitimized social relationships. Even slaveowners, who should have known better, tended to use their own yardsticks to measure the kin arrangements of their slaves. Cheryl Ann Cody, who has studied the naming patterns of the slaves in South Carolina, recently concluded that the majority of the slaves "conceived of their families in a broad sense, including extended kin," while their owners "saw the nuclear family as the primary unit."[26] Along these lines, a former Louisiana slave recalled that "in our family am pappy, mammy, and three brudders and one sister, Julia, and six cousins."[27]

Under the circumstances, it may even be somewhat misleading to use the term *family* to describe all of the variegated kin relationships that African-born slaves created in the early years, particularly during the long first century. The same could be said, with appropriate qualifications, about some members of the creole population in later years. *Family* is probably inappropriate because it conjures Western images of a male, a female, and their children, living in a union sanctioned by the church or the state. The relationships that the enslaved created, often without Christian sanction and certainly without state approval, ran the gamut of what would be characterized in contemporary Western terms as *monogamy, polygyny,* or *consensual unions.* We should avoid homogenizing such diverse kin relationships under a narrowly constructed and general rubric with an attendant Western connotation.

In many important respects, the majority of African-born slaves understood the meaning of a union between a male and a female quite differently from their more Westernized and creole counterparts. For most Africans, the primary relationship in a marriage was between the two lineages from which the partners hailed. The relationship between the husband and the wife was secondary precisely because of the transcendental importance of kinship obligations and the precedence of the needs of the community over those of individuals.

Generally speaking, the fundamental purpose of marriage was to produce children, thereby increasing the size of the group and enlarging the network of kin relationships. Parenthood was ascribed a special meaning and value because it meant the fulfillment of the highest obligations to the community as a whole. Consequently, fertility was highly prized and infertility could constitute appropriate grounds for the annulment of the marriage. Since the procreative aspect of the relationship was all-important, women of childbearing age were at a premium and tended to be offered for sale less frequently than the men. Childless and unmarried women failed to fulfill their culturally assigned roles and expectations and probably became pariahs. Polygyny was one appropriate response in those societies at times when there was a numerical superiority of women.

Since the bond that united the man and the woman was secondary to that which cemented the two lineages, the parents of the couple and the elders of the community played the principal roles in spousal choices. They initiated the discussions concerning the union, decided on its timing, the gifts that accompanied it, and the ceremonies that gave it legitimacy. Some of these societies had patrilineal descent systems, while others were matrilineal.

Under patrilineal systems the children of the marriage belonged to the father's kin; they belonged to that of the mother in matrilineal practice. The problem of descent is of paramount importance in such societies, because it determines the distribution of property. The wife's kin inherit the estate under matriliny, while the father's kin are the recipients under patriliny. Such societies are characterized as unilineal, in contrast to those that are bilineal, with descent flowing from both males and females.

It is important to keep the nature of Africans' traditional kin arrangements in mind when examining the evolution of family life under slavery. Their violent removal from their ethnic group destroyed the web of kin relationships that anchored them and secured their societal place. The resulting kinlessness must have exacerbated their emotional pain and despair in ways we can never begin to understand. To be without kin was to be the perpetual outsider, to be socially dead. Parents and community elders were not present with the African captive in America to determine spousal choices in those situations where marriageable partners were available. We may also guess that when marriages occurred they were not usually accompanied by the customary ceremonies, given the absence of kin and appropriate authorities.

The systems of patriliny and matriliny also broke down as a consequence of the slave trade and slavery. During the long first century, Africans were never present in significant numbers to recreate these crucial aspects of their lives. In addition, individuals who were socialized into one system or the other probably found themselves in the same household or on the same farm, further complicating the problem of cultural reconstruction. In any event, most slaves possessed little if any property to bequeath to their kin. Then, too, slave marriages lacked legal standing in America, so the partners were afforded none of the legal protection, such as inheritance rights, that the law gave to white couples. Louisiana legislators found it necessary to remind residents of the state in 1824 that "Slaves cannot marry without the consent of their masters, and their marriages do not produce any of the civil effects which result from such contract."[28]

Although African-born slaves could not recreate — except with considerable difficulty — their traditional domestic and kin arrangements, it is certain that the memory of these and other aspects of their heritage survived and were transmitted in modified forms to their descendants. In fact, the moorings and sensibilities of traditional Africa were reflected in the high premium placed on fertility, the ways in which a new birth was celebrated, naming patterns, the unqualified respect accorded elders, the nature of burial rites, and the sanctity of kin ties. These and other African-inspired practices and sensibilities continued to inform life throughout the period of slavery and beyond.

Whatever their nature, however, the evidence is clear that blacks developed a network of relationships as soon as chance, the demographic situation, and the sex ratio facilitated it. The emergence of these ties of kin and non-kin should not be seen primarily as acts of resistance to the dehumanizing efforts of the master class. Rather, they represented the perfectly normal expressions of their humanity and their conscious desire to recreate kinship systems and social relationship to help give meaning to their lives. The variety of the systems they created tell us much about their efforts to define themselves and to order their intimate lives according to their own rules.

We now turn to the question of the religious beliefs and organizations of the enslaved. Slave societies of the Americas have been noted for the vitality and exuberance of their religious practices. While this has evoked much comment and even admiration, the roles that the multiplicity of religious beliefs and practices played in the quarters have never been satisfactorily explained, at least from the standpoint of the practitioners. In many instances, contemporary scholars, often Christians themselves, have viewed the religious behavior of African slaves through Christian lenses, an approach that distorts more than it reveals. The challenge is to determine the actual religious beliefs of American slaves over time and to understand how they shaped behavior, morals, values, and world views.

This is no easy task under the best of circumstances. But it becomes more complex when one tries to understand the belief systems of other peoples in the past, particularly those who left few written records about such matters. From a theoretical and methodological standpoint, it is also necessary to understand these beliefs on their own terms and avoid seeing Christianity as the norm or the standard against which they should be measured. We must appreciate the fact that Africans came from societies with deeply held religious beliefs and traditions. Christians did not normally respect these beliefs and some of them thought that it was their duty to convert Africans. Such a position, of course, was rooted in the ethnocentric notions of Western cultural and religious superiority.

The contemporary historian and reader must avoid such pitfalls. We must abandon Western and Christian biases in reconstructing the religious history of the peoples of African descent. In other words, we should not start with the assumption that what Christianity had to offer was superior to what the African religions represented. Not only does such a position interfere with our understanding of the African peoples and their religions, but it often leads us to criticize slaveowners and representatives of Christian denominations for neglecting the souls of the Africans. Western historians have frequently done this because of their assumptions, usually not recognized, that Christianity was a "good thing" for the African peoples. Such a seemingly theological position has no place in a historical discussion of the beliefs of the slaves, to say nothing of the perverse judgment of African cosmologies that it conveys. We should also not confuse the role of Christianity in contemporary black America with that which it played at an earlier time, nor should we minimize the meaning and implications of religious conversion for the African-born.

The peoples who came to North America from West and West Central Africa brought with them a coherent set of religious ideas and practices. Their societies had developed elaborate and complex cosmologies long before the start of the slave trade. Although many of the ethnographic sources upon which we rely for information on African traditional religions lack historical depth and depict them in a static, timeless fashion, certain generalizations can be cautiously advanced. First, African religious ideas cannot be meaningfully isolated from those that inform economic, political, and social life. They are part of a tightly woven fabric of interrelated ideas that explain the origins of the universe and the nature of humans, and connect them to the worlds of the living and the dead. Their cosmologies explain evil and misfortune, establish codes of behavior, and elucidate the relationship of human beings to the Supreme Being. All of these societies have highly systematized rituals and archetypal symbols or sacred images. In addition, there is a hierarchy of religious specialists such as priests, prophets, and diviners.

In spite of considerable variations in the nature of these beliefs and in their expression, there was a common set of principles, broad cores of understandings, that appear to have transcended ethnic boundaries. Most of these societies accepted the concept of a Supreme Being and believed in lesser gods, ancestor worship, and the efficacy of spirits. Similarly, their cosmologies tended to make no distinctions between the religious and the secular aspects of life. Religious beliefs both shaped and were reflected in their art, music, dance, and world-views. One's private and social identity was inextricably bound up with one's religious beliefs and heritage.

Seen in this light, to divest Africans of their religious beliefs would be, in effect, to destroy their core, their personhood. The African-born who embraced Christianity underwent a transfiguration, with all of its awful and awesome consequences. It meant a remaking of oneself, a state that few would achieve. It may be argued, of course, that the transformational leap for Christianized Africans was not as wide as this argument implies, since there were similarities between Christian beliefs and those of the Africans.

Such a claim may not be without merit, but it is risky, nonetheless. African religious behavior was shaped, conditioned, circumscribed, and legitimized by a whole series of rituals that had profound meanings in their particular context. Ceremonies imposed meanings on an activity, artifact, or practice. Thus, the ceremonial context was all-important: nothing had any meaning unless it was conferred by the appropriate rituals and by those empowered to do so. Beneath the apparent similarities to Christianity, more complex principles and meanings often functioned. Thus, African beliefs and practices cannot be abstracted from their cultural settings, and perceived similarities to Christian practice may obscure more than they reveal. No scholar would seriously maintain that European Christians confused the deeper meanings and symbolism of their cross with that used by the Bakongo, but somehow the reverse is repeated by several authorities, perhaps betraying Western condescension toward African beliefs, their meanings, and intensity.

The forced African immigrants, then, brought highly complex belief systems that had served them well. Scattered across the colonies in that long first century, it must have been difficult for them to find meaningful religious expression and interaction. Many rituals had to be performed collectively, and a priest or some other religious authority had to be present to do the honors. Other activities took place only in sacred places with objects that possessed special meaning and efficacy. In some cases, only the priests knew the religious secrets and determined the moment for their revelation and expression. None of this could be recreated in their new setting, at least not easily. For a people whose lives were built around ceremony and ritual and who drew strength from their religious practices conducted in a particular setting, they must have experienced a spiritual death. Not until their numbers increased were they able to reconstruct the broad contours of their beliefs, and even this would have been exceedingly difficult.

The records are silent on the private pain of these Africans, uprooted and bereft of the psychic balm that a community-centered religion helped produce. Being separated from kinfolk added to their emotional burden and sense of profound loss. In such a state, Africans were likely to blame their misfortune on themselves, on some transgression that had brought forth such punishment. Some would have questioned the power of their own deity, who had failed to protect them from such adversity. In their despair, as Monica Schuler has shown for African immigrants in Jamaica, some probably came to accept the white man's sorcery and magic—that is, his religious power—as superior to their own.[29]

Such recognitions of the superior power of the white man's sorcery helps explain some Africans' receptivity to Christianity. On another level, it may also be surmised that Christianity would appeal to those who, having lost everything, sought to reorganize their lives in a new land. Christianity gave structure to their emotional and spiritual thrashings even as it exacted its own price.

Unlike some of the existing studies, we must recognize that for Africans, conversion to Christianity meant that they had to reject much of their past assumptions and beliefs, a difficult process given the integrated nature of the religious and the secular. According to the African scholar, John M'biti, conversion to Christianity would mean a fundamental change in the African's interior being, his "thought patterns, fears, social relationships, attitudes and philosophical disposition."[30] The African would undergo a metamorphosis and emerge as a new person with an altered sense of identity. The individual, in other words, would have experienced a transfiguration.

Understandably, many Africans resisted this process, and historians now know that only a small minority of the African-born converted to Christianity during slavery. Even many of the creoles, who were in the numerical ascendancy in the nineteenth century, remained untouched by Christian ministrations.[31] Probably only about one-fourth of the slave population was Christian by 1865. It is becoming relatively clear that Christianity achieved its most enduring successes among the black population after Emancipation. If that is the case, previous conclusions about the Christian or sacred world of the slaves need to be revised. Similarly, if only a minority of the slaves were touched by Christianity before Emancipation, our attention as historians should be focused not so much on the ethnocentric question of how "Christianized" the slaves were — as if that were the norm for them — as on the religious beliefs and practices of the many who embraced other options.

We need to rethink the view that what emerged in the quarters was essentially a syncretic combination of African religious traditions and Christian beliefs. I would argue instead that the African-born slaves who became Christians incorporated Christian theology into their existing belief systems, reinterpreting it and transforming it in the process. This new complex of beliefs — an emerging Afro-Christianity — met some of their spiritual needs, but it did not generally replace core African beliefs, nor did it always suffice. In fact, Africans continued to express a profound faith in the efficacy of their charms, rituals, and religious principles, even as they sought the comforting ministrations of a Christian clergyman.

This situation is not astonishing; human beings have the capacity to integrate concepts into their belief systems that appear contradictory to the outsider. The often repeated proposition that Africans did not understand much of what the Christians taught them may only be partially correct. Two belief systems, in time, came to coexist. On the one hand, there was a dynamic, ever-evolving blend of African and Christian beliefs that can be called Afro-Christianity. On the other, there were African core beliefs that remained beyond the reach of Christian influences. That which was given primacy depended upon the needs of the moment. Accordingly, our efforts to understand the texture of religious life in the quarters should not be centered simply on whether African slaves were Christianized, the nature of their Christian or traditional beliefs, or the degree of syncretism that occurred. Rather, we should recognize a dynamic, complex, and constantly transforming set of beliefs — at once coherent, at once contradictory — that defies any dogmatic characterization.

There are obviously other aspects of the lives of the slaves that need to be reviewed. We need a more nuanced understanding of the childhood experiences of the creoles, with a view to understanding the forces that shaped their adult personalities. Their cultural assumptions and practices need to be explored with greater sensitivity and less romantic condescension. Above all, we should undertake a serious and dispassionate assessment of the nature of that intellectual revolution associated with slavery studies. We cannot remain prisoners of old paradigms, nor can we cease the intellectual sifting and winnowing that is at the heart of our craft. There cannot be a single controlling interpretation of that complex institution of slavery, to be sure. But twenty years after Fischer wrote, we need new questions, new understandings, new answers, and new debates.

NOTES

1. I shall refrain from criticizing scholars by name in this paper. Careful students of the historiography of slavery will be able to associate the ideas that I criticize with their most articulate proponents.
2. David Hackett Fischer, *The New Republic*, 2 (Dec. 9, 1978): 30.
3. Richard Hofstadter, "U. B. Phillips and the Plantation Legend," *Journal of Negro History*, 29, no. 2 (Apr., 1944): 124.
4. For a fine discussion of early Iberian attitudes towards Africans, see James Hoke Sweet, "The Iberian Roots of American Racism," M.A. thesis, University of North Carolina at Chapel Hill, 1995. See also Sylvia Wynter, "The Eye of the Other: Images of the Black in Spanish Literature," in *Blacks in Hispanic Literature*, edited by Miriam DeCosta (Port Washington, New York: Kennikat Press, 1977), pp. 1–17; A. J. R. Russell-Wood, "Iberian Expansion and the Issue of Black Slavery: Changing Portuguese Attitudes, 1440–1770," *American Historical Review*, 83, no. 1 (Jan., 1978): 16–42; William McKee Evans, "From the Land of Canaan to the Land of Guinea: The Strange Odyssey of the 'Sons of Ham'," *American Historical Review*, 85, no. 1 (Jan., 1980), 15–43; David Eltis, "Europeans and the Rise and Fall of African Slavery in the Americas: An Interpretation," *American Historical Review*, 98, no. 1 (Jan., 1993): 1399–1423.
5. St. Clair Drake, *Blackfolk Here and There*, volume 2, (Los Angeles: University of California Press, 1990), pp. 243–44.
6. A. C. De C. M. Saunders, *A Social History of Black Slaves and Freedmen*

in Portugal, 1441–1555 (London: Cambridge University Press, 1982), p. 166.

7. Ibid., p. 167.

8. Ibid., p. 39.

9. Ruth Pike, *Aristocrats and Traders: Sevillian Society in the Sixteenth Century* (Ithaca, New York: Cornell University Press, 1972), p. 174.

10. Ibid., pp. 187–88.

11. Frederick Pike, ed., *Latin American History: Select Problems* (New York: Harcourt, Brace and World, 1969), pp. 46–47.

12. For a discussion of this issue see Pierre Van den Berghe, *Race and Racism: A Comparative Perspective* (New York: Wiley, 1967).

13. Wynter, "The Eye of the Other," p. 15.

14. Ronald Sanders, *Lost Tribes and Promised Lands: The Origins of American Racism* (Boston: Little, Brown, 1978), p. 52.

15. Anthony Padgen, *The Fall of Natural Man: The American Indian and The Origins of Comparative Ethnology* (Cambridge: Cambridge University Press, 1982), pp. 15–16.

16. John Parry and Robert Keith, eds., *New Iberian World: A Documentary History of the Discovery and Settlement of Latin America to the Early Seventeenth Century,* volume 1 (New York: Times Books, 1984), pp. 290–322.

17. Padgen, *The Fall of Natural Man,* p. 33.

18. Ibid., p. 33.

19. David Brion Davis, *The Problem of Slavery in Western Culture* (Ithaca, New York: Cornell University Press, 1966), p. 53.

20. McKee Evans, "From the Land of Canaan," p. 29.

21. Padgen, *The Fall of Natural Man,* p. 32.

22. The best analysis of the development of racial slavery in North America during the seventeenth century is found in Alden T. Vaughan, *Roots of American Racism: Essays on the Colonial Experience* (New York: Oxford University Press, 1995).

23. Peter Wood, *Black Majority: Negroes in Colonial South Carolina from 1670 through the Stono Rebellion* (New York: W. W. Norton, 1974); Russell R. Menard, "The Maryland Slave Population, 1658 to 1730: A Demographic Profile of Blacks in Four Counties," *William and Mary Quarterly,* 32 (Jan., 1975): 29–54; Alan Kulikoff, *Tobacco and Slavery: The Development of Southern Cultures in the Chesapeake, 1680–1800* (Chapel Hill: University of North Carolina Press, 1986).

24. Slavery and racism also had a profound effect on the psychology of whites and corroded the institutions of the society. This issue merits serious study.

25. Monica Schuler, *"Alas, Alas Kongo": A Social History of Indentured African Immigration into Jamaica, 1841–1865* (Baltimore: Johns Hopkins University Press, 1980).

26. See Cheryl Ann Cody, "Slave Demography and Family Formation: A

Community Study of the Ball Family Plantations, 1720–1896," Ph.D. dissertation, University of Minnesota, 1982.

27. Ann Patton Malone, *Sweet Chariot: Slave Family and Household Structure in Nineteenth Century Louisiana* (Chapel Hill: University of North Carolina Press, 1992).

28. James Oakes, *Slavery and Freedom: An Interpretation of the Old South* (New York: Alfred A. Knopf, 1990).

29. Schuler, *"Alas, Alas Kongo"*, pp. 33–36.

30. John M'biti, *African Religions and Philosophies* (New York: Praeger, 1970), p. 146.

31. On these questions see Albert Raboteau, *Slave Religion: The 'Invisible Institution' in the Antebellum South* (New York: Oxford University Press, 1978); and Mechal Sobel, *Trabelin' On: The Slaves Journey to the Afro-Baptist Faith* (Westport, Conn.: Greenwood, 1979).

"He Is an African But Speaks Plain":

Historical Creolization in Eighteenth-Century Virginia

DOUGLAS B. CHAMBERS

Two slaves named Bob and Bristol ran away from the home plantation of their master, John Hartwell Cocke of Surry County, in April, 1774. After crossing the wide James River and making their way to Williamsburg, they were caught and taken to Cocke's kinsman in that town for interrogation. Bob and Bristol had succeeded in getting Cocke to write a pass for them "by the Plausibility of their Story," even though Bristol was described as "an outlandish Fellow." Bristol and Bob cooperated in their scheme to run away in the direction of the colony's capital because each needed the other to better his chances for escape. Together, this fugitive team represented the Janus-face of historical creolization in eighteenth-century slave culture.[1]

Bob was a mixed-race ("mulatto") man who had worked as a fer-ryman on the James River for many years. His observation of and inter-actions with the white planters he carried on the ferry, or what Bob's master termed his "Acquaintance with Gentlemen," had taught Bob the personal characteristics required for a slave to pass as a free man, among which were "an immoderate Stock of Assurance" and the ability to be "artful, designing, and exceedingly smooth tongued."[2] Bristol, on the other hand, looked and acted like the quintessential slave — an unassimilated African, or "new Negro."[3] Cocke considered Bristol to be "as ignorant as [Bob] is artful." He also assumed that the two would stay together, and that the outlandish Bristol would "entirely submit to, and confide in, his Companion's Counsels."[4]

Runaway slave advertisements are replete with examples of such cooperation across the cultural spectrum of eighteenth-century slave community life. More importantly, however, the published notices and other evidence speak to the fact of a creolization continuum in early Virginia, and to the enduring influence of africanisms in the historical development of Afro-Virginian slave culture.[5] Historical creolization resulted in a cultural continuum, and in Virginia, as elsewhere in the New World, American-born slaves continued to find much of use in the cultures of their African-born parents and grandparents.

White slave owners recognized that their slaves were a heterogeneous lot, with some slaves more or less "black," more or less proficient in English, more or less "outlandish," and more or less "pleasing" than others. And yet, even the most assimilated slaves showed clear evidence of a separate, African-oriented, creole cultural influence. For example, in 1784 Landon Carter described an extraordinary slave of his named General as one who spoke English "readily, and without restraint, seeming to aim at a stile above that generally used by slaves." Carter went on to qualify his praise, however, by noting that there was "something corrupt" in General's English style. Two years later an Albemarle County planter described his own runaway mulatto slave, Joe, as "a good Barber, and a handy fellow about a Gentleman's person, being always kept as a waiting-man," and yet he mentioned, in passing, that the mixed-race Joe "speaks broken English."[6] Other mulattos in the mid–1780s were as African in appearance and personal style as "new Negroes," such as an unnamed Charlotte County mulatto slave woman who ran away in 1784, and who was described as "outlandish, and has some of her country marks on one of her cheeks."[7] Another mulatto man, Dick, the waiting-man of George Mason of Fairfax County, was "artful and plausible [and] beats a drum pretty well."[8] In short, many Virginia-born slaves spoke a distinctive creole English and appeared to be distinctively non-European, even as many other slaves who were born in Africa learned sufficient English to "speak plain."

Slaves in eighteenth-century Virginia created a distinctive creole culture. As the numbers of people grew and the proportion of Africans in the slave population declined, they and their immediate descendants fashioned a hybrid society that, because of the importance of family relations, on the one hand, and the conflict-ridden relationship between slaves and masters, on the other, remained heavily African-influenced. Slaves valued their black kin and feared their white masters. They also found strength in numbers, especially in the densely populated "black belt" of the interior tidewater and fall-line counties, where Afro-Virginians constituted a clear majority of the population. The relatively large size of slave-holdings there, the tendency to create kin-based (rather than territorial-based) communities, and the creation of an ethical system based on slave honor, or what I call *honorance,* rather than on Christianity encouraged slaves to draw on African cultural resources as they adapted to the conditions of slavery in Virginia.[9] The historical Afro-Virginian world that the slaves made apart was based on a heritage as much African as American.[10]

The decades of the 1760s and 1770s were the key years in this historical process of creolization. A rapidly growing population had created a "creolization continuum," with roughly equal numbers of people demonstrating distinctively African patterns of personal style as those who approximated the behavior of whites. This continuum, measured by linguistic creolization (proficiency in spoken English), remained stable in the second half of the century. There was no single rush to speak the King's English, and slaves neither simply lost nor had their African heritages "stripped away."[11] As late as 1790, Africans who could not speak any English or who could speak it only "brokenly" were quite visible, and they were running away from their owners as often as slaves who spoke English fluently.[12] There also were more and more Virginia-born slaves like Bob, who understood the connection between an Anglo-Virginian personal style and one's chance to pass as free. What tied these two ends of the slave creole continuum together and constituted the shared mind behind the Janus-face of early Afro-Virginian society and culture was honorance.

The twin issues of how and why Africans became something new — what we call African American today — in the New World has been an implicit theme in much of the history of slavery in the Americas. An earlier generation of historically oriented sociologists and anthropologists sought, largely in response to the overtly racist assertions of an even earlier generation of Southern historians, to explain the "loss" of African material and community cultures in the New World in terms of a more or less coercive process of "acculturation."[13]

Both Melville Herskovits and E. Franklin Frazier began with the assumption that blacks were a despised minority forced to live among whites, and that they suffered for it; both men spent their lives studying how African Americans solved "the business of living in this culture which is not his own."[14] But whereas Frazier emphasized the damage done to black society and culture, arguing that the means of enslavement and the conditions of the Middle Passage and plantation life were so brutal as to strip away the African heritage of the slaves, Herskovits described a process of change from initial contact to acculturation and assimilation.[15] Even though Herskovits heroically attempted to document the "Africanisms" still extant in various twentieth-century African American communities, his acculturation model aimed at explaining the relative loss of most forms of African society and culture in the New World by defining a "scale of intensity . . . from most to least African" and by rank-ordering contemporary societies in terms of this typology of loss.[16]

In the 1950s and 1960s historians often entered these debates with polemical works that sought to validate either Frazier's or Herskovits' position.[17] Later, two seminal books that launched the "community-studies" approach, Gerald Mullin's *Flight and Rebellion: Slave Resistance in Eighteenth-Century Virginia* (1972) and John Blassingame's *The Slave Community: Plantation Life in the Antebellum South* (1972), each attempted to split the difference between Frazier and Herskovits by showing how resistance and assimilation went hand in hand. Both Mullin and Blassingame, however, concluded their studies by emphasizing the eventual assimilation of acculturated slaves to white cultural and social norms.[18]

In the 1970s and 1980s historians shifted to a new model of culture-change, creolization, which they derived from formal linguistic theory. Rather than focusing on how Africans "lost" their cultures in their new social contexts, creolists sought to explain how Africans "remade themselves" in the New World.[19] These emphases on creative adaptation and the concept of culture as a social construction succeeded in moving the debate beyond the increasingly stale search for African survivals (retentions, transformations, and so on), on the one hand, or the supposed pathology of damaged and maladaptive African American social/cultural forms, on the other. In other words, as Sidney Mintz and Richard Price wrote, "the Africans in any New World colony in fact became a *community* and began to share a *culture* only insofar as, and as fast as, they themselves created them."[20] The modern creolization model gave historians a new vocabulary for discussing social and cultural development, and they subsequently produced a flood of brilliant monographs.[21]

Sidney Mintz and Richard Price attempted to describe systematically a program for the comparative study of African American creolization from an anthropological perspective. Building on their assertion that immigrant generations of Africans did not share a common language, and thus that they tended to constitute "crowds" or "aggregates" of people rather than "groups," they attempted to explain, first, how such strangers created an ad-hoc or improvised set of simplified institutions (akin to a pidgin or trade-language), and second, how their children elaborated these arrangements into a fully formed creole culture.[22] Their method was anthropological because of the distinction they drew between institutions (social-relational arrangements, or syntax) and style (cultural norms and aesthetics, or grammar), and because the explicit end of comparative analysis was to explain the present.[23]

Their basic interpretive point was that immigrant African slaves on plantations throughout the New World initially had little or nothing in common other than their enslavement—they were all strangers in a strange land. The cultural heterogeneity of West and West-Central Africa and the randomizing effects of the transatlantic slave trade meant that these new slaves did not constitute a speech-community, nor did they share common institutional forms (other than in the abstract, such as unilineal descent) or specific cultural styles. Mintz and Price argued that among these immigrant crowds the only constant was change, and that, in fact, all slave societies demonstrated an "integral dynamism."[24] They argued that slaves expected to experiment and that rapid social and cultural change was the norm, beginning with new institutions such as the "shipmate bond" and bilateral descent, new languages (pidgin first, then creole), and new religions (often syncretistic). In their view, local conditions were determinative in defining these ad-hoc solutions to the new conditions the slaves faced. In the end, there were very few "direct formal continuities" with old ethnic-African institutions, yet slaves somehow succeeded in extending or preserving much of the style of their disparate African heritages.[25]

As compelling as this anthropologically oriented model is, there are a number of problems for historians. The first is the orientation of the basic theoretical position toward the present. While the present obviously flows from the past, it also conditions what the modern poet Howard Nemerov has termed "the cantilevered inference," out of which we make our perception of the past.[26] More importantly, Mintz and Price's heuristic emphasis on the initial immigrant moment, the point furthest removed in time from the present, encourages a simplistically unilinear, evolutionary, or historicist understanding of any one region's history. This is why Mintz and Price seem confused by post-Emancipation shifts in gender roles, for example, and why even the most subtle applicators of their method still end up emphasizing assimilation.[27]

In recent years, historians have begun to critique the bases of Mintz and Price's formulation of the creolization thesis. Taking advantage of the flood of quantitative studies of the transatlantic slave trade that gave historians better control over the question of the coastal origins of Africans sent to various New World regions and colonies and in the process asking much more detailed questions of traditional documentary sources, historians have returned to considerations of the contributions of Africans in the development of African American cultures.[28]

In his sweeping reappraisal of the sixteenth and seventeenth centuries, John K. Thornton argued that the peoples of West and West-Central Africa were much less culturally heterogeneous, and the transatlantic slave trade was much less random than had been previously thought. Using language families as metaphors for cultural types, he suggested that there were three "culturally distinct zones" and seven sub-zones from which the vast majority of Africans came, and that the process of enslavement in Africa and subsequent dispersal in New World colonies tended to "concentrate, rather than disperse" peoples of similar cultural zones.[29] Most importantly, many Africans in the New World would have met enough speakers of their mother-languages to have constituted speech-communities from the beginning, so that Africans would not have had to "start from scratch culturally upon their arrival in the New World."[30] Fragmentary evidence from the Caribbean suggests that many Africans in the early centuries of the transatlantic slave trade tended to gravitate toward others of the same "nation," and that they rapidly established communities "that could develop and transmit their culture."[31]

Gwendolyn Midlo Hall's monograph on colonial Louisiana, though concerned largely with the history of slave resistance and rebellion under the French and Spanish regimes, supports in vivid detail the main points of Thornton's general critique. She documents that two-thirds of the nearly six thousand slaves imported into Louisiana under the French (1719–43) came from Senegambia and that many of these people were either Bambara or were heavily Mande-influenced.[32] These slaves constituted a "language community" in colonial Louisiana, and the creole culture they created showed clear and sustained evidence of their influence.

Although Thornton and Hall both use colonial Virginia as a case in contrast,[33] the anthropological formulation of the creolization thesis does not work for eighteenth-century Afro-Virginia either. The transatlantic slave trade to the Chesapeake was not random, but instead tended to concentrate Africans from a few regions, especially Igbo-land in present-day southeastern Nigeria (the coast of which was known to Europeans as "Calabar"). During the first half of the eighteenth century, nearly fifty percent of all Africans forcibly transported to Virginia originated in the Bight of Biafra. In the crucial first three decades (1704–30), the proportion of Igbo in Virginia's import-trade approached sixty percent. Between 1704 and 1745, moreover, Virginia planters imported three times as many Igbo as they did any other African ethnic group. Over the course of the eighteenth-century slave trade, I estimate that at least twenty-five thousand Igbo wound up in Virginia, representing forty percent of all forced migrants brought to the colony directly from Africa.[34]

The decades of the most intensive importation of Africans (1710–40) were also the years that white planters tended to send "new Negroes" to settle newly claimed land in the colony's piedmont region, which would have concentrated even further the numerically dominant African ethnicities in Virginia. Africans on such backcountry quarters — even those on the owners' home plantations — would have found enough linguistically similar others to constitute a speech-community.

Between 1717 and 1720, for example, one major importer of slaves (John Baylor of King and Queen County, on the middle reaches of the Mattaponi River, near Walkerton) had a hand in selling the slave cargoes of at least fourteen separate shipments totalling nearly twenty-one hundred slaves. Fully seventy-five percent of those people came from the coast of Calabar and would have been mostly Igbo.[35] One of Baylor's sub-factors, Ambrose Madison, bought two adult women in 1721 from a Calabar cargo, and two years he later co-patented nearly five thousand acres in western Spotsylvania County. In late 1725 or early 1726 Madison purchased eight more slaves (probably newly arrived Africans, most likely Igbo, as well) and "seated" the patent-lands prior to moving there in the late 1720s. At Madison's death in 1732, only five of his twenty-nine slaves were adult women (with ten adult men and fourteen children); perhaps this is why the only child to have a distinctively afrophonetic name (Cussina) was a girl, as was the only child named after an adult (Nancy).[36] In any case, if the two women purchased from the same ship in 1721 survived their first decade to be recorded in Madison's probate inventory, then they (like many other enslaved women in the region) would have produced children and thereby established a community whose African American members were heavily Igbo-influenced.

Many Africans in colonial Virginia were likely to constitute groups rather than crowds, and thus individuals could effectively reconstitute speech-communities. Such Africans in Virginia were surrounded with fellow exiles rather than by complete strangers. One white missionary recognized this fact when he tried to Christianize Africans in mid-eighteenth century Virginia. He exhorted them to

> not only pray for your Country-men, who are with you in America, but likewise pour out your very Souls to God in Prayer for all the Inhabitants of your own Native Land. Tho' you are now removed to such vast Distance from them, yet your Prayers will reach them.[37]

Most Africans in eighteenth-century Virginia did not need to create a pidgin language to communicate with each other and therefore probably did not rely on ad-hoc social and cultural solutions to situations that they faced in common. Instead, we can imagine women like the two from "Calabar," who, sharing not just a common Igbo (or Igbo-ized) culture but also the special bond of having survived the Middle Passage on the same ship, found themselves owned by the same man. These women did not need a pidgin to talk with each other, but they did need a lingua franca (Plantation Creole) to communicate with their master and mistress and other whites (and perhaps other blacks in the neighborhood). When purchases of new slaves enlarged the group, these women would have served as translators (in eighteenth-century parlance, "linguisters"), and their children would have grown up learning both the mother-tongue and Plantation Creole. The use of an English-based lingua franca was the result of historical rather than anthropological creolization and was the basis of the creolization continuum so evident throughout eighteenth-century Afro-Virginia.

Plantation Creole was part of a speech continuum from broken to plain to fluent English. Professor J. L. Dillard and other modern creolists argued that this continuum represented the life-cycle of pidgin/creole languages. The phenomenon can also be seen in terms of a "dynamic wave theory," with immigrant Africans radically reducing or reforming English in the process of acquiring it as a second language. Succeeding generations then expanded this "indigenized language" into Plantation Creole, but within a diglossic or ethnic/immigrant speech environment. Immigrants and their children would have shared a domestic language for private communication, while using Plantation Creole for wider public communication. The "best" speakers, or those considered "very fluent" by whites, perhaps represented linguistic decreolization or the achievement of a creole slave *koine*, which approached the standard colonial American dialect of English.[38]

Although Hugh Jones noted in 1724 that slaves who were born in Virginia "talk good English, and affect our Language, Habits, and Customs," many other observers testify to the fact that throughout the century numerous Afro-Virginians had "imperfect Acquaintance with our Language."[39] John Davies wrote in the 1750s that, when preaching to slaves, "I often lower my style in my Sermons, and address them in a plain and pathetic manner." In a sermon preached at Hanover Courthouse in 1757, Davies argued against the presumably commonly held proposition that most Afro-Virginians were "so stupid, or so ignorant of our Language, that it may be impossible to teach them."[40] In 1784, J. F. D. Smyth noted that many Afro-Virginians spoke "a mixed dialect between the Guinea and the English."[41] Describing his experiences in the last quarter of the century, the well-travelled Baptist preacher, John Leland, wrote that "their language is broken, but they understand each other, and the whites may gain their ideas."[42] As late as 1830, one could come across a group of slaves, as Frederick Douglass did in Maryland, who could barely speak English. Douglass remembered that the group he observed spoke "a mixture of Guinea and everything else you please. . . . I could scarcely understand them, so broken was their speech."[43]

Africans also influenced the speech of whites. In 1736, an English traveller criticized Anglo-Virginians for allowing their children "to prowl among the young Negroes, which insensibly causes them to imbibe their Manners and broken Speech."[44] Sixty years later, Johann Schoepf noted of his travels in post-revolutionary Virginia that

> the salmagundy of the English language has here been enriched even by words of African origin, and some of these are regarded as really meritorious additions, e.g., the negro expression *"toat"*, to carry something on the shoulders, for which there is no word in the English.[45]

Although technically a dialect and not a true creole (in that Plantation Creole was largely intelligible to speakers of Standard English), the speech of slaves was distinctive and clearly showed the effects of African substrate influence.[46] A late eighteenth-century example of "plain" Plantation Creole in the Chesapeake region is presented in a 1792 serial novel, in which an African-born Maryland slave is invited to give an oration before "The Philosophical Society" about finding "an Indian's petrified moccasin." He begins:

> Massa shentiman; I be cash crab in de Wye riva: found ting in de mud; tone, big a man's foot: hols like to he; fetch Massa: Massa say, it be

de Indian Moccasin. — O! fat de call it; all tone. He say, you be a fila-safa, Cuff: I say, O no, Massa, you be de filasafa. Wel; two tree monts afta, Massa call me, and say, You be a filasafa, Cuff, fo' sartan: Getta ready, and go dis city, and make grate peech for shentima filasafa.[47]

An example of "plain" slave English from the 1770s was recorded by the master of a slave named Richmond. The slaveholder had sold another slave because he had "scarcely understood a single word that I said to him, nor did I know one syllable of his language." Presumably Rich-mond's English was more intelligible:

Kay, massa, (says he), you just leave me, me sit here, great fish jump up into de canoe, here he be, massa, fine fish, massa; me den very grad; den me sit very still, until another great fish jump into de canoe; but me fall asleep, massa, and no wake till you come; now, massa, me know me deserve flogging, cause if great fish did jump into de canoe, he see me asleep, den he jump out again, and I no catch him so, massa, me willing now take good flogging.[48]

One can hear clear echoes of this eighteenth-century "plain English" in the speech of some antebellum Virginia slaves. In 1835 one writer observed that, when questioned about whether they would like to be purchased, slaves often responded (perhaps ritually) with something on the order of "Massa good massa, me no like to leave him — no leave massa."[49] A northern traveller who bought two recently transported Virginia-born slaves in Mississippi in 1835 recorded this plea from one of them:

Young master, you never be sorry for buy George; I make you a good servant. But — beg pardon, master — but — if master would be so good as buy Jane. . . . My wife, since I come from Wirginny. She good wife and a good girl — she good seamstress an' good nurse — make de nice shirts and ebery ting.[50]

Just after Emancipation, one slave in Augusta County rejected the reli-gious overtures of a young white minister with the statements, "I jus' let 'ligion go" and "You Met'dis blind leadin' de blind."[51] Thomas Wentworth Higginson, writing of the Christian-influenced songs his black soldiers sang during the Civil War, noted that "Sometimes they substituted 'hinder *we*' [for 'hinder me'], which was more spicy to the ear, and more in keeping with the usual head-over-heels arrangement of their pronouns." An example of just such an arrangement is an indirect quote from a slave in Botetourt County, talking about his African-born father: "Den sometimes at night he would say: *'He gwine sing he country'*, den he would dance and jump and howl and skeer us to death."[52]

Historical creolization and the consequent creole cultural continuum in Virginia occurred within the social context of a rapidly growing black population. The slave population more than doubled between 1720 and 1740, doubled again in a mere fifteen years, and by the 1780s there were nearly three-hundred thousand enslaved descendants of Africans in Virginia. The black population, which had been growing by physical reproduction (through "natural increase") since the 1730s, continued to do so in the early national period. In 1790 Afro-Virginians accounted for over forty-four percent of all black people in the South. Even though tens of thousands of people left Virginia for newly opened lands in Kentucky, Tennessee, and Alabama in the 1790s and early 1800s, Afro-Virginians still made up one-third of Southern blacks in 1810 (see Tables I, II).[53]

TABLE I: VIRGINIA SLAVE POPULATION, 1680–1820[54]

Year	Accepted Estimate	Other Estimates	
1680	3,000		
1690	9,350		
1700	16,390		
1710	19,350	3,118	
1720	26,550		
1730	36,600	30,000	
1740	60,000		
1750	107,100	101,452	
1755	120,000	127,650	
1760	140,550		
1770	187,600		
1780	220,600		
1782	229,088		
1790	292,627	293,427	292,717
1800	346,968	345,796	
1810	392,518		
1820	425,153		

The early and sustained physical creolization or "natural increase" of the slave population meant that African-born slaves comprised an ever smaller proportion of black people in Virginia. In the 1720s over half of

TABLE II: VA. BLACK POPULATION (SLAVE AND FREE), 1755–1820[55]

Year	Number	Pct./South
1755	120,000	—
1790	305,393	44%
1800	367,092	40%
1810	423,088	33%
1820	462,042	28%

the adult population had been brought from Africa within the previous ten years; by 1750 the proportion of African-born slaves had fallen to about a third, and only about fifteen percent of slaves had come from Africa within ten years. In the piedmont region, Africans accounted for as much as sixty percent of the slaves in the 1750s, but for only ten to twenty percent by 1782.[56]

Fragmentary evidence for over fifteen hundred slaves mentioned in runaway advertisements suggests that the proportion of African-born slaves in Virginia declined dramatically during the mid-eighteenth century.[57] In the 1740s and 1750s, owners mentioned the birth provenance of two-thirds of their fugitive slaves, presumably because that fact mattered much at the time. Of those with a provenance given, some thirty-seven percent were African-born. In the 1770s and 1780s about two-thirds of the slaves were listed without a birth provenance, presumably because that fact no longer mattered very much. The proportion of African-born slaves in those latter decades, about seventeen to twenty-two percent, dovetails with the conventional population estimates, and over three-quarters of the fugitive slaves with a given provenance were "country-born" (see Tables IIIa, IIIb).

Even though the proportion of Africans in the slave population declined dramatically over the course of the eighteenth century, linguistic evidence suggests that the creole cultural continuum remained remarkably stable. Moreover, the evidence for linguistic creolization, drawn as it is from runaway slave advertisements in Virginia papers, probably overstates the general proficiency of slaves in English, since the slaves whose personal style most closely approximated that of the whites tended to run away most often. In general, though, between the 1730s and 1790 about one-third of runaway slaves spoke broken or "bad" English, one-third spoke plain or "good" English, and the other third either spoke English fluently or with the accent of other European languages or English dialects. Most importantly, this continuum, from

TABLE IIIA: GENERAL PROVENANCE OF FUGITIVE SLAVES, 1736–1790[58]

Year	Not Given	African-Born	Va-Born	Other-Born
1736–57 N = 143	35%	24%	37%	4%
1761–74 N = 623	50%	11%	36%	3%
1775–90 N = 108	62%	6%	29%	3%

TABLE IIIB: SPECIFIC PROVENANCE OF FUGITIVE SLAVES, 1736–1790

Year	African-Born	Va-Born	Other-Born
1736–57 N = 93	37%	57%	6%
1761–74 N = 623	22%	72%	6%
1775–90 N = 303	17%	76%	7%

broken to plain to fluent, did not shift significantly toward fluency with the physical creolization of the slave population in Virginia. The proportion of those slaves who showed the most "substrate" (African) influence in their speech actually increased in the 1760s and then declined in the following two decades. But they still accounted for nearly thirty percent of the runaways advertised in the years of the revolutionary crisis and its aftermath (see Tables IVa, IVb).

Clearly, in the second half of the eighteenth century, the steady decline in the proportion of African-born people in the slave population did not translate into a unilinear shift from broken to fluent English among Afro-Virginians. In other words, the creole linguistic continuum remained stable even though more and more of the slaves were born and raised in Virginia. Physical creolization, therefore, did not automatically

TABLE IVA: LINGUISTIC CREOLIZATION CONTINUUM, 1736–1790

Year	broken/ Bad	plain/ Good	fluent/ Very Good	Other
1736–57 N = 56	32%	43%	23%	2%
1761–74 N = 150	39%	32%	29%	1%
1775–90 N = 109	29%	38%	28%	5%

TABLE IVB: COMPARATIVE LINGUISTIC CREOLIZATION

1766–84 N = 229	34%	34%	30%	3%
1736–90 N = 315	34%	36%	28%	3%

result in linguistic assimilation. Instead, the process of historical creolization created a linguistic continuum with continuing African influence.

The stability of the linguistic creolization continuum among slaves over time suggests that, contrary to most historians' current interpretation, African influence in late eighteenth-century Virginia was not "a constantly dwindling one."[59] Many Afro-Virginian slaves demonstrated a strong substrate influence in their speech, so that rapid physical creolization caused no marked shift in the linguistic continuum. In addition, physical creolization did not translate into a wholesale shift towards assimilating white expectations of submissive or docile behavior among the slaves.

The non-random nature of the transatlantic slave trade and the ability of Africans to find and reconstitute ethnic speech combined with a third factor to encourage Africans to draw on their ethnic cultures in adapting to life in Virginia: most slaves had only limited and conflict-ridden interactions with their white masters. Slaves lived in separate dwellings and dealt with whites largely in terms of work or punishment. Daily interaction with whites was limited and often induced visible fear, discomfort, and even strange involuntary behaviors among individual slaves.

Whites were often brutal and cruel in their interactions with slaves. Slaveholders tended to enforce their power through physical means—often branding, cropping ears, cutting off limbs, or severely whipping or scourging their slaves for both imaginary and real crimes. In a letter to an overseer in 1727, Robert "King" Carter offhandedly suggested that the overseer get a court order to cut off the toes of a recalcitrant runaway, claiming, "I have cured many a negro of running away by this means."[60] In the 1770s travellers to Virginia noted that slaveholders' "authority over their slaves renders them vain and imperious"; that whippings were "often very severe, and sometimes desperate"; and that, as St. George Tucker argued after the turn of the century, "it is the natural consequence of tolerating slavery to harden the heart in cruelty."[61] In the 1780s another visitor to Virginia remarked on the "laborious and harassing life the negroes lead in this country," and a North Carolina planter wrote in 1802 that "there is no such thing as having an obedient and useful Slave, without the painful exercise of undue and tyrannical authority."[62]

Philip Vickers Fithian, after being hired as a tutor for the children of Robert Carter of Nomini Hall, wrote in his diary in 1773 the torture technique of one of Carter's overseers:

> For Sulleness, Obstinacy, or Idleness, says he, Take a Negro, strip him, tie him fast to a post; take then a sharp Curry-Comb, & curry him severely til he is well scraped; & call a Boy with some dry Hay, and make the Boy rub him down for several Minutes, then salt him, & unlose him. He will attend to his Business, (said the inhuman Infidel) afterwards![63]

Thomas Jefferson's famous dictum that "the whole commerce between master and slave" was a "perpetual exercise of the most boisterous passions, the most unremitting despotism on the one part, and degrading submissions on the other,"[64] while largely accurate regarding whites, misses the mark somewhat with blacks. A contemporary slave saying from late eighteenth-century South Carolina—"when Mossa curse, he break no bone"—better evokes the response of many slaves to the tyranny of slaveholders.[65] Or, as a man who had been born in Old Calabar and raised in New York later remembered, "From my observations of the conduct and conversation of my master and his sons, I was led to hate those who professed themselves Christians, and to look upon them as devils."[66]

Throughout the eighteenth century many slaves resisted meaningful interaction with their white masters, as many contemporary reports confirm. In 1752 a Goochland County slave named Jack was described as having "a down cast sly Look when spoken to." Another Goochland County slave named Jack, who ran away in 1766, "speaks plain for an African born, but avoids looking in the Face of them he is speaking to as much as possible." A mulatto woman named Kate in the 1770s had "a down look when she talks." A 1784 advertisement for a Caribbean-born mulatto man named Lewy claims that he "generally hangs his head when spoken to."[67]

As with historical linguistic creolization, descriptions of the general "appearance" or "character" of runaway slaves reveal a continuum from what whites considered "bold" or "impudent" to "downcast" to "pleasing" countenances. Like the linguistic continuum, this behavioral one remained largely stable over the century.[68] Whites continued to characterize blacks as "such sullen perverse Creatures, or stupid Dunces, that it is impossible to teach them any Thing that is good,"[69] suggesting that many slaves attempted to maintain clear psychological boundaries and to deal with whites—when they were forced to interact with them—largely on their own terms.

Again, the evidence is fragmentary, but runaway slave advertisements suggest that in the second half of the century physical creolization did not result in cultural assimilation. Between 1736 and 1790 about half of the slaves consistently maintained either a sullen or a boldly impudent personal style when dealing with their masters, with only about one-third interacting with any kind of habitual congeniality. Fully one in five of the 303 runaway slaves whose advertisements included a character judgment exhibited fear-based involuntary behaviors, such as stammering or involuntary bodily movements. In the 1760s and 1770s (as well as earlier, although the evidence is skimpier), Afro-Virginians tended either to maintain an uncomfortable interpersonal mask or to react in fear when interacting with whites, and the proportion of those enslaved people whose interactions with their masters were thoroughly and habitually negative and conflict-ridden remained much the same in the post-revolutionary years (see Table V).[70]

For many other slaves, any interaction with whites was so frightening that it induced involuntary behaviors, often noted in advertisements. The owner of a Virginia-born Louisa County slave named Pompey noted in 1766 that the runaway was "very apt to wink his eyes quick, contract one corner of his mouth, and stammer in his speech when under any apprehensions of fear." In the 1770s a Williamsburg

TABLE V: SLAVE/WHITE INTERACTIONS CONTINUUM, 1736–1790[71]

Year	A.	B.	C.	D.
1736–57 N = 20	20%	35%	15%	30%
1761–74 N = 141	30%	31%	14%	25%
1775–90 N = 142	32%	33%	21%	14%
1736–90 N = 303	31%	32%	17%	20%

man named Billy exhibited a "remarkable turning of his eyes and winking, with some hesitation before he replies upon being spoken to." In the 1780s a Cumberland County man named Samuel, "when spoken to, often turns his head on one side, and shuts one of his eyes, but which it is I do not remember." An Orange County woman named Scisley "when spoke to is very huffy, and is remarkable in shewing the whites of her eyes." In general, between 1775 and 1790 perhaps twenty-five percent of the Virginia slaves described in such advertisements responded in clearly distressed and fearful ways to interactions with their master (and presumably, with other whites as well).[72]

Increasingly, however, Afro-Virginians found strength in numbers. As their population increased dramatically in the eighteenth and early nineteenth centuries, creolizing slaves created a distinctive "black belt" in Virginia, where they constituted a clear majority of the resident population. A superficial tabulation of gross population statistics, however, has lead to the assumption that black people in Virginia were always a distinct minority, generally amounting to about forty percent or less of the state's population. The reality of historical creolization was much different.

As a number of historians have documented, there was a rapid shift in the slave population from the tidewater areas to those in the piedmont region, where the slave population was increasingly concentrated.[73] The most dramatic shift occurred in the generation before the Revolution, but the pattern continued in the following decades, so that by 1820 nearly two-thirds of the slaves lived in the lands between the fall-lines of the rivers and the Blue Ridge mountains.

TABLE VI: VIRGINIA SLAVE POPULATION
BY MAJOR REGION[74]

Year	Tidewater		Piedmont		Transmontane	
	No.	Pct.	No.	Pct.	No.	Pct.
1755	79,197	66%	39,599	33%	1,200	1%
1782	105,380	46%	116,835	51%	6,873	3%
1790	128,795	44%	149,286	51%	14,636	5%
1800	124,465	36%	197,734	57%	24,769	7%
1810	120,753	31%	229,148	58%	42,617	11%
1820	122,105	29%	259,601	61%	43,447	10%

More importantly, however, during the third quarter of the eighteenth century a "black belt" developed in the interior counties along the fall-lines of the region's major rivers. The slave populations in counties ranged along the Mattaponi, Pamunkey, Chickahominy, and Appomatox rivers all experienced rapid and sustained growth, especially between the 1750s and 1780s. In the 1780s Afro-Virginians constituted a majority of nearly sixty percent in these black-belt counties, and the black majority increased its proportion of the region's population in the early national era. A visitor to a plantation in Essex County in 1785 noted that "There are 1,500 acres of land here . . . and an amazing number of Negroes, and a great many small houses to lodge them."[75] In about 1805 Robert Sutcliff, a Quaker, described the area to the north-east of Falmouth (across the Rappahannock from Fredericksburg) with the succinct statement that "the population of this part of the country consisted chiefly of black people." His travels from Richmond to Goochland led him through "extensive plantations, cultivated by negro slaves, many of whom dwell in small clusters of huts, at no great distance from their master's house."[76]

Within this black-belt region, the Mattaponi/Pamunkey watershed (whose population "fed" the settlement of the central piedmont between the James and Rappahannock rivers), and the Appomatox river watershed (which was the entrepot for the southern piedmont) were the two areas of greatest black population growth, and with the largest black majorities, even in the decades of out-migration (see Tables VII and VIII). By the 1780s, then, about two out of every three people in the black-belt region were the descendants of Africans.

Historical creolization in Virginia was both the cause and the consequence of relatively large average slaveholdings there, especially in the

TABLE VII: VIRGINIA "BLACK-BELT" POPULATION[77]
(Upper York and Upper James river valleys)

Group	1755	1790	1800	1810	1820
Total	93,684	172,709	166,667	168,443	185,332
Black	46,252	100,809	99,700	103,529	113,006
White	47,432	71,900	66,967	64,914	72,326
% Black	49.4%	58.4%	59.8%	61.5%	61%

TABLE VIII: DYNAMIC "BLACK BELT" POPULATION
(Mattaponi/Pamunkey and Appomattox Rivers watersheds)

Group	1755	1790	1800	1810	1820
Total	75,112	136,926	135,363	135,775	151,504
Black	37,560	80,203	81,144	83,948	90,172
White	37,552	56,723	54,219	51,827	58,760
% Black	50%	59%	60%	62%	60%

black-belt region where Afro-Virginians were already a clear majority of the population. Whereas Allan Kulikoff argued that most slaves in the Chesapeake lived in holdings too small either to constitute fully formed communities or to afford the enslaved people with much autonomy, slaves in Virginia's black belt area, at least, tended to live on significantly larger plantations. In general, whereas almost three-quarters of the slave-masters owned five or fewer slaves, nearly three-quarters of enslaved people were owned in groups of eleven or more.

The vast majority of slaves, especially in the interior counties in the third quarter of the century, lived in larger groups; over forty-two percent of the slaves were owned in holdings of twenty-one or more (see Tables IX, X, and XI). Fully three-quarters of Afro-Virginians in the black-belt area in 1782 were owned in groups large enough to constitute one to eight quarters, that is, in groups of six to forty-nine, and more slaves lived on the largest plantations (holdings of fifty or more) than the whole number of slaves who were owned in the smallest-sized group (five or less). As Morgan and Nicholls noted for the piedmont, "most of the region's slaves lived on plantations of sufficient size to support a measure of community life."[78]

The numbers documenting the interior region's black majority and

TABLE IX: SIZE OF SLAVEHOLDINGS, COMBINED BLACK-BELT, 1782[79]

| | Slaveholders | | Slaves | |
Avg. Size	No.	Prct.	No.	Prct.
1–5	1,930	48%	5,026	13%
6–10	957	24%	7,460	19%
11–20	693	17%	10,044	26%
21–49	390	9%	11,285	29%
50+	69	2%	5,266	13%
Total	4,039		39,081	

TABLE X: COMPARATIVE SIZE OF SLAVEHOLDINGS

| | Slaveholders | | Slaves | |
Avg. Size	No.	Prct	No.	Prct.
6–49	2,040	51%	28,789	74%
21+	459	11%	16,551	42%

TABLE XI: SLAVEHOLDINGS, MATTAPONI RIVER REGION

| | | Slaveholders | | Slaves | |
	Avg. Size	No.	Prct.	No.	Prct.
A.					
	1–5	732	46%	1,938	11%
	6–10	370	23%	2,863	17%
	11–20	296	18%	4,360	26%
	21–49	180	11%	5,213	31%
	50+	33	2%	2,641	15%
	Totals	1,611		17,015	
B.					
	6–49	846	53%	12,436	73%
	21+	213	13%	7,854	46%

the relatively large size of slave-holdings there only underscore the importance of kith and kin to the historical development of Afro-Virginia slave culture. Enslaved Africans and their creole descendants built their communities on the twin foundations of kin (or the centrality of family) and slave honor (corporate social esteem). Of course, these two primary principles of historical slave culture — the importance of family (*kinful-ness*) and the expression of slave honor (honorance) — were directly related,[80] both the core and the product of the African-centered process of historical creolization in Virginia.

The demographic and social contexts of slavery in early Virginia encouraged the formation and reproduction of family life among the slaves. Rather than making the family "insecure and precarious," the contingency of slavery and the African-oriented nature of Afro-Virginian slave culture encouraged the valorization of family as an institution of community life.[81]

Some contemporary white people recognized that slaves in colonial and early national Virginia placed great weight on the importance of family and the social relations of kin connections in their community and individual lives. James K. Paulding, writing about his experiences in the summer of 1816, argued that the threat of separation by sale made slaves value their family ties more than did whites: "it is seldom we see the ties of kindred or of conjugal affection, stronger than in the poor negro. He will travel twelve, fifteen, or twenty miles, to see his wife and children. . . . If he obtains his liberty, he will often devote the first years of his liberty, to buying their freedom." William N. Blane, an Englishman who travelled through the region in 1822, wrote that "The Blacks are in general very quiet people, and are uncommonly fond of their children."[82] Letitia Burwell, the mistress of a antebellum family plantation where the slaves' roots extended back to the colonial black-belt, recalled that "The Old negroes were quite patriarchal; loved to talk about 'old times', and exacted great respect from the Young negroes."[83]

In the eighteenth century a surprising number of white slave-owners recognized the reality of paternal kin relations among the slaves. Clearly, Afro-Virginian social sanctions for or cultural affirmation of slave father-hood had not been subsumed by the master class's dictum of *partus sequitur ventrem* (status follows that of the mother), which had been the law since 1662.[84] From the 1760s to the 1780s at least eleven fugitive slave advertisements mentioned slaves as fathers. In 1769 a woman named Venus was described as "the daughter of a slave called Jemmy, a cooper." A slave named John ran away from his master in Williamsburg, who suspected that John had gone to Warwick County, "where he has a father and grandmother, and other relations." In 1787 Jack of Essex County, described as "outlandish, and speaks broken English," was expected to head for his former owner's plantation, "where he has several children."[85]

Over the course of the century, as physical creolization increased the slave population, Afro-Virginians turned more and more to family for support and for solidarity. Their masters increasingly took these family relations into account, especially when imputing motivations and supposed destinations of escaped slaves. In the second quarter of the century, very few slaveholders thought of their slaves' kin networks when they advertised for runaways. From the 1760s through the 1780s, however, about one in six of all such advertisements included some mention of the slaves' conjugal, nuclear, or extended family (see Table XII). After 1760, moreover, forty-one percent of the nearly six hundred advertisements with owner-supplied motivations suggested that the runaway might intend to return to old haunts, follow relatives, or "lurk" where they had kin to harbor them.[86]

TABLE XII: KIN TIES AMONG RUNAWAYS, 1736–1790[87]

Year	A.	B.	Y.
1736–57	2	3	5
Total 111	2%	3%	5%
1761–74	57	19	76
Total 503	11%	4%	15%
1775–90	90	19	109
Total 610	15%	3%	18%
1761–90	147	38	185
Total 1,113	13%	3%	17%

In fact, it seems more productive to think about historical slave communities in terms of kin networks (a function of family), rather than in terms of territory (a function of white ownership and plantation boundaries). Slaves created and maintained a number of institutions—including "abroad marriages," fictive kinship (signified by honorifics such as *Aunt* and *Uncle*), and customary visiting rights—in order to expand the range of their interpersonal contacts and relationships. Slaves were not confined to the people whom their masters owned; they created their own networks of consanguinal and affinal ties that bound them one to another across the physical landscape.

Many of those ties and relationships were cast in an African-oriented mold and were informed by the ethos of honorance. As in any slave society, Afro-Virginians labored under a state of generalized dishonor.

Individual slaves could achieve recognition for their talents, character, and personal rectitude, and thereby garner a certain amount of respect from individual whites, but as a class, slaves were people without honor. Johann Schoepf captured this dichotomy perfectly when he observed that "A traveller on foot is in Virginia an uncommon spectacle; only negroes go a-foot; gentlemen ride." He went on to note that "the whole country being made up of gentlemen and their negroes, and almost no other distinction obtaining, it is always something extraordinary to meet a white foot-traveler."[88]

White conceptions of honor as a moral code or ethical system revolved around the public claim to and performance of exalted self-worth. As one modern Southern historian has so succinctly put it, in the antebellum South (white) honor was "a system of values within which you have exactly as much worth as others confer upon you."[89] Esteem and respect accrued to those who were honored. A white adult male exacted and defended such esteem through the threat or reality of violence and reproduced it through personal bravery, sumptuary and competitive display, oath-taking, and conviviality, all in terms of "his understanding of who he is and where he belongs in the ordered ranks of society."[90]

In the world of eighteenth-century Virginia, where to be black brought the presumption of slave status, Africans and their descendants could hardly avoid knowing their status in the ranks of a society ordered by whites. Afro-Virginians, however, drew on their own cultural resources to create a distinctive system of slave honor based on the idea of honorance. For slaves, the ideal of righteous behavior — including respect for elders, dignified conduct, protecting the weak, supporting the strong, taking care of one's own, and punishing disrespect, all very "African" values — privileged the action of honoring as well as the condition of being honored. Slave honor was bivalent, because esteem accrued to those who would "treat everybody right." Like whites, though, slaves enforced their system of honor through personal and social sanctions, including violence.[91]

The performance of honorance had four basic components — personal display, pride (and its obverse, shame), vengeance (violence), and group loyalty — all of which were clearly operating to define the world that Africans and their descendants made apart in colonial Virginia.[92] Personal display was more than bodily ornament; it also included competence in skilled performance, such as drumming, dancing, singing, gaming, and story-telling. Country marks and teeth-filing (scarification), coiffures (especially among women), and wearing finery or brown-colored wigs are other examples of this component.[93]

Pride often had to do with a slave's general demeanor; it was exhibited in those who were habitually bold and impudent, as well as by those who tended to be downcast. A Spotsylvanian slave named Jack, described in 1779 as "outlandish," also tended to wear a cap in order "to hide one ear that is cropt on the top." An Albemarle slave man named David was described in 1784 as a "proud trafficking fellow"; another slave in the 1780s was "of a proud carriage."[94]

Vengeance, or the enforcement of honor through violence, was also common. Some historians have tended to interpret violence among slaves in eighteenth-century Virginia as a function of internal divisions, especially the supposed hostility between African-born and creole slaves.[95] Most violence among slaves, however, was an expression of breached honor; it included poisoning, conjuring, and such "Southern" phenomena as gouging, maiming, and "wrasslin."[96] A British officer who had been paroled to Albemarle during the Revolution wrote that the slaves were "continually poisoning each other, thro' disappointment, or jealousy: what is remarkable, they can administer the poison that it shall affect the life for a longer or a shorter period, agreeable to their ideas of revenge on the object."[97]

Some vengeance took the form of threats; others actually resulted in attacks on slaveholders, as when a Williamsburg slave named Foy ran away in 1777 after beating his overseer; another slave named Emanuel, owned by the same man, "laid violent hands" on his owner, "dashed [him] on the ground," and then ran off. Although such offenses brought immediate outlawry, with slaveholders offering large sums of money for the killing of such slaves (or smaller amounts if the person was brought back alive), they were far from uncommon. A Northumberland slave named Mann threatened to burn down his master's houses in 1768, ran off, and was outlawed for it. His owner advertised that he was willing to pay a ten-pound reward to any person who would "deliver me his head, severed from his body"; if returned alive the owner would pay only two pounds. A 1769 advertisement warns that a slave from King and Queen named Ben had a reputation for being fierce, as he had "formerly made several overseers fear him."[98]

The most ubiquitous form of honorance, however, was the harboring of runaway and other slaves by their family, friends, acquaintances, and relations. Such group loyalty could take the form of refusing to inform on another person or dissembling in order to protect oneself and others from masters. Sometimes group loyalty extended to saving someone from the very clutches of their masters and overseers. Two Cumberland slaves were rescued in 1771 by a group of fellow slaves in Albemarle County when they "violently [took them] away from my overseer."⁹⁹

The constituent importance of group loyalty to slave honor, and of slave honor to slave culture, helped to unite enslaved people at either end of the Afro-Virginian creole continuum; it also helped slaves to see each other as potential sources of support in a social system that condoned the oppressive circumstances of racial slavery. Heavily African-influenced slaves such as John Hartwell Cocke's Bristol, who certainly would have understood the language of honorance, could rely on slaves such as the mulatto ferryman Bob because both shared a common interest, a common culture, and created their own bonds of trust in a world they made apart from whites. Slave honor bound them to each other, and historical creolization was the process by which they drew on African resources to adapt to life in Virginia.

In the last years of the Revolution, the openly racist French officer the Marquis de Chastellux echoed a note of caution he must have picked up while in the new Commonwealth of Virginia. Around 1780 he noted that Afro-Virginians were so numerous as to "equal at least, if they do not exceed, the number of white men" in Virginia and worried that these slaves were becoming a "distinct people" and inherently a threat to white honor and republican order: "Necessarily united by interest, by the conformity of their situation, and the similarity of colour, they would [if freed] unquestionably form a distinct people, from whom neither succour, virtue, nor labour, could be expected."¹⁰⁰

Ever perceptive, Thomas Jefferson expressed his own reservations concerning the future of a new nation he helped found. His judgment clouded somewhat by his own visceral racism, Jefferson prophesied irreconcilable differences among free and slave, white and black, arising from the "deep rooted prejudices entertained by the whites; ten thousand recollections, by the blacks, of the injuries they have sustained." Jefferson prophesied that this Manichaean conflict between the members of what clearly had become two very different worlds — one inhabited by free white people and the other by enslaved black people — would "probably never end but in the extermination of the one or the other race."¹⁰¹

Such a sentiment could not have resonated in a world that white and black had made together. In fact, the African-oriented creole world that the slaves made apart in eighteenth-century Virginia was tangible proof of quite another sentiment, offered by a London merchant travelling through Virginia in the 1780s: "one half the world do not know how the other half live."[102] In eighteenth-century Virginia, as elsewhere in African America, the ways the slaves lived reflected the African influences of the historical culture they created in their creole world.

NOTES

I would like to thank the following for their comments, constructive criticisms, and support: Joseph C. Miller, Edward L. Ayers, John M. Hemphill II, Gail Terry, Stephen Innes, the Carter G. Woodson Institute for African and Afro-American Studies at the University of Virginia, and the members of the Southern History Seminar, Corcoran Department of History, University of Virginia.

1. Lathan A. Windley, comp., *Runaway Slave Advertisements: A Documentary History from the 1730s to 1790,* volume 1 (Westport, Ct.: Greenwood Press, 1983), pp. 146–47.
2. Ibid.
3. In the colonial era the terms *African, saltwater Negro, new Negro, outlandish,* and *wild* were all roughly equivalent; see Philip D. Morgan, "British Encounters with Africans and African Americans, circa 1600–1780," in *Strangers within the Realm,* edited by Morgan and Bernard Bailyn (Chapel Hill, 1991), pp. 199–200.
4. Winley, *Runaway Slave Advertisements,* pp. 146–47.
5. A continuum of creolization, from outlandish to new Negro to acculturated to assimilated slaves, is implicit in Gerald W. Mullin's *Flight and Rebellion: Slave Resistance in Eighteenth-Century Virginia* (London: Oxford University Press, 1972), but he emphasizes the rapidity of assimilation. The final sentence of his seminal work reads, "Slavery in the nineteenth century would be based on a heritage more American [read white, Christian] than African" (p. 163). In *Water From The Rock: Black Resistance in a Revolutionary Age* (Princeton: Princeton University Press, 1991), a recent attempt to make Christianity the core of African American slave culture, Sylvia P. Frey emphasized the early and "systematic repression of the African heritage." While acknowledging the prevalence of such African social forms or "cultural survivals" as polygyny and mud-walled houses, she wrote, "Under the constraint of constant surveillance by the plantation system, much of the African cultural heritage was, of course, lost" (pp. 27–36).

6. Winley, *Runaway Slave Advertisements,* pp. 370, 384.
7. Ibid., p. 374. This example is especially important, since her "country" was presumably colonial Virginia. She was born circa 1749, and one of her parents was probably African, since he or she scarified her in the style of an African ethnic group.
8. Winley, *Runaway Slave Advertisements,* p. 362.
9. Slave honor as an ethical system was first developed in John Willis' essay in *The Edge of the South,* edited by Willis and Edward L. Ayers (Charlottesville, 1991), pp. 37–55. By *honorance* I mean the obsolete eighteenth-century sense of the word: the idea that esteem accrues to the performer of honor as well as to the one honored; as in the *OED* citation of "As honour is in honourance, in him that honours rather than in him that is honoured." It is interesting that this word went out of use in British English in the eighteenth century.
10. Compare with Mullin, *Flight and Rebellion,* p. 163; Allan Kulikoff, "Uprooted Peoples," in *Slavery and Freedom in the Age of the American Revolution,* edited by Ira Berlin and Ronald Hoffman (Charlottesville: University Press of Virginia, 1983), pp. 153–54.
11. The latter position is most forcefully argued in E. Franklin Frazier *The Negro Church in America* (Liverpool: University of Liverpool, 1963); Stanley M. Elkins, *Slavery: A Problem in American Institutional and Intellectual Life* (Chicago: University of Chicago Press, 1959).
12. Winley, *Runaway Slave Advertisements,* p. 419.
13. See Robert W. Fogel, *Without Consent or Contract: The Rise and Fall of American Slavery* (New York: Norton, 1989), pp. 154–75; Uhlrich Bonnell Phillips, *American Negro Slavery: A Survey of the Supply, Employment and Control of Negro Labor as Determined by the Plantation Regimes* (New York: Appleton, 1918); Melville J. Herskovits, *The Myth of the Negro Past* (New York: Harper, 1941); and Frazier, *The Negro Church.*
14. Herskovits, *The American Negro: A Study in Racial Crossing* (New York: Knopf, 1928), p. 54.
15. Frazier, *The Negro Church,* pp. 9, 11; Herskovits, *The Myth of the Negro Past.* See also Herskovits, *Acculturation: The Study of Culture* (Gloucester, Mass.: Peter Smith, 1958), pp. 1–32; and Herkovits, *The New World Negro: Selected Papers in Afroamaerican Studies* (Bloomington: Indiana University Press, 1966), pp. 12–23, 43–61.
16. Herskovits, *The New World Negro,* pp. 51–55.
17. The most obvious example is Elkins, *Slavery,* third revised edition (1976), pp. 267–302; but see also Kenneth Stampp, *The Peculiar Institution: Slavery in the Antebellum South* (New York: Vintage, 1956), pp. 141–91, 322–82.
18. For Mullin, the issue was occupational mobility (assimilation brought "better" jobs); for Blassingame the key was Christianization (Mullin,

Flight and Rebellion, pp. 161–63; Blassingame, *Slave Community*, pp. vii–ix).

19. Sidney Mintz and Richard Price, *The Birth of African-American Culture: An Anthropological Approach to the Afro-American Past* (Boston: Beacon Press, 1992), p. 84.

20. Minz and Price, *Birth of African-American Culture*, p. 14.

21. Including Herbert G. Gutman, *The Black Family in Slavery and Freedom 1750–1925* (New York: Vintage, 1976); Mechal Sobel, *Trabelin' On: The Slave Journey to an Afro-Baptist Faith* (Westport, Ct.: Greenwood, 1979); Charles Joyner, *Down By The Riverside: A South Carolina Slave Community* (Urbana: University of Illinois Press, 1984); Kulikoff, *Tobacco and Slaves*, pp. 317–51; Sobel, *Made Together;* and Margaret Washington Creel, *"A Peculiar People": Slave Religion and Community-Culture among the Gullahs* (New York: New York University Press, 1988). For the clearest statement, see Joyner, *Riverside*, pp. xix–xxii, 203–207.

22. Mintz and Price, *Birth of African-American Culture*, p. 18.

23. Ibid., pp. 83–84.

24. Ibid., pp. 42–51.

25. So that, for example, kinship and gender roles were highly contingent; Ibid., pp. 52–80; quote, p. 60.

26. "The Makers," in Howard Nemerov, *Trying Conclusions: New and Selected Poems, 1961–1991* (Chicago: Chicago University Press, 1991), p. 94.

27. Mintz and Price, *African-American Culture*, pp. 74–80; Sobel, *Made Together,* passim. See also Charles Joyner, "'One People': Creating an Integrated Culture in a Segregated Society: 1526–1990," in *The Meaning of South Carolina History: Essays in Honor of George C. Rogers, Jr.,* edited by David R. Chesnutt and Clyde N. Wilson (Columbia: University of South Carolina Press, 1991), pp. 243–44.

28. Two important studies are John K. Thornton's *Africa and Africans in the Making of the Atlantic World, 1400–1680* (Cambridge: Cambridge University Press, 1992), and Gwendolyn Midlo Hall's *Africans in Colonial Louisiana: The Development of Afro-Creole Culture in the Eighteenth Century* (Baton Rouge: Louisiana State University Press, 1992).

29. Thornton, *Africa and Africans*, pp. 186–99; quote, p. 205.

30. Ibid., pp. 212–16.

31. Ibid., p. 163. For an excellent summary statement, see pp. 204–205.

32. Hall, *Africans in Colonial Louisiana*, pp. 29–55, 60.

33. Thornton, *Africa and Africans*, pp. 165–66, passim; Hall, *Africans in Colonial Louisiana*, p. 161.

34. The numbers are derived from Walter Michinton, Celia King, and Peter Waite, eds. *Virginia Slave-Trade Statistics 1698–1775* (Richmond: Virginia State Library, 1984). "Angolans" (KiKongo and KiMbundu) accounted for about one-fifth, and "Gambians" (Mande) for some fifteen percent, with Gold Coast (Akan) and Madagascar (Malagasy)

each about seven percent, and Windward Coast (Mende/Mande) about four percent.

35. See Baylor Papers, series 4, Baylor Ledgers 1719–1744, volume 1, Alderman Library, University of Virginia, acc. #2257. Of the 2,094 slaves imported, 1,554 were from "Calabar" (74%), 340 from Madagascar (16%), 136 from "Africa" (7%), and 64 from "Barbados" (3%), although internal evidence in Minchinton, et. al., *Slave-Trade Statistics* would suggest that both of the last two shipments originated on the coast of Igboland as well (pp. 41–49).

36. Baylor Ledgers; Douglas B. Chambers, "The Making of Montpelier: Col. James Madison and the Development of a Piedmont Plantation, 1741 to 1774," M.A. thesis, University of Virginia, 1991, pp. 22–32.

37. Benjamin Fawcett, *A Compassionate Address to the Christian Negroes in Virginia* (London, 1756), p. 26.

38. J. L. Dillard, *Black English: Its History and Usage in the United States* (New York: Random House, 1972), pp. 84–86; Robert A. Hall, *Pidgin and Creole Languages* (Ithaca, N.Y.: Cornell University Press, 1966), pp. 126–27, 130–35; Dell Hymes, ed., *Pidginization and Creolization of Languages: Proceedings of a Conference Held at the University of the West Indies, Mona, Jamaica, April 1968* (Cambridge: Cambridge University Press, 1971); Albert Valdman *Pidgin and Creole Linguistics* (Bloomington: Indiana University Press, 1977); John A. Holm, *Pidgins and Creoles*, volume 1 (Cambridge: Cambridge University Press, 1988), pp. 8–9, 52–60.

39. Hugh Jones, *The Present State of Virginia* (1724), p. 37, 38, 71; also Samuel Davies, *The Duty of Christians to Propagate their Religion* (London, 1758), p. 34.

40. Samuel Davies, *Letters from the Rev. Samuel Davies* (London, 1757), p. 37; Davies, *The Duty of Christians*, p. 44.

41. Quoted in Dillard, *Black English*, p. 88.

42. John Leland, *The Virginia Chronicles* (Fredericksburg, Va., 1790), p. 13.

43. Quoted in Blassingame, *Slave Community*, p. 27.

44. Quoted in Sobel, *Made Together*, p. 137.

45. Johann Schoepf, *Travels in the Confederation [1783–84]*, translated and edited by Alfred J. Morrison (New York: Bergman, 1968), p. 63.

46. For analyses of historical Black American English see John R. Rickford, "The Question of Prior Creolization in Black English," in Valdman, ed., *Pidgins and Creole Linguistics*, pp. 190–221; Dillard, *Black English*, pp. 73–109; Salikoko S. Mufwene, ed., *Africanisms in Afro-American Language Varieties* (Athens: University of Georgia Press, 1993).

47. Hugh Henry Brackenridge, *Modern Chivalry* (1792), pp. 115–16. A Standard English version of the opening paragraph would be:

Gentlemen masters; I was catching crabs in the Wye river; and found the thing in the mud; a stone, big as a man's foot; it had holes like one; fetched Master; Master said, it is an Indian moccason; Oh, that's what you call it; it's all stone. He says, you are a philosopher, Cuff: I said, O no, Master, you are the philosopher. Well; two or three months afterwards [later], Master called me, and said, You are a philosopher, Cuff; for certain: Get you ready, and go to this city, and make a great speech for the gentlemen philosophers [there/here].

48. Quoted in Dillard, *Black English,* pp. 87–88.

49. Ethan Allen Andrews, quoted in Willie Lee Rose, *A Documentary History of Slavery in North America* (New York: Oxford University Press, 1976), p. 373.

50. Joseph Holt Ingraham, quoted in Rose, *Documentary History,* p. 167.

51. Solomon L. Conser, *Virginia after the War. An Account of Three Years' Experience in Reorganizing the Methodist Episcopal Church in Virginia at the Close of the Civil War* (Indianapolis: Baker-Randolph, 1891), pp. 72, 75.

52. Thomas Wentworth Higginson, quoted in Rose, *Documentary History,* p. 478; Letitia Burwell, *Plantation Reminiscences* (N.p.: Page Thacker, 1878), p. 8 [my emphasis].

53. Allan Kulikoff, "A 'Prolifick' People: Black Population Growth in the Chesapeake Colonies," *Southern Studies* (1977): 394, 412; for out-migration see Kulikoff, "Uprooted Peoples," in Berlin and Hoffman, *Slavery and Freedom.*

54. The numbers for the Accepted Estimates [AE] before 1782 are rounded. Sources for AE 1680–1700, 1720, 1740, 1760–1780 are from Census Bureau, *Historical Statistics of the United States* (Washington, D.C., 1975), p. 1168. AE for 1710, 1730, 1750 from Kulikoff, "'Prolifick' People", p. 415; AE for 1755 from Robert E. and Katharine Brown, *Virginia 1705–1786: Democracy or Aristocracy?* (East Lansing: Michigan State University Press, 1964), pp. 73a–73b; AE for 1782 from Morgan and Nicholls, "Slaves in Piedmont Virginia," p. 218. AE for 1790–1820 are from U.S. Census, *Return of the Whole Number of Persons* (Washington D.C., 1800); U.S. Census, *Aggregate Amount of Persons Within the United States* (Washington D.C., 1811); U.S. Census, *Census for 1820* (Washington D.C., 1821). The Other Estimates [OE] sources for 1710, 1730, 1750 are from *Historical Statistics,* p. 1168; OE for 1755 from Kulikoff, "'Prolific' People," p. 416.; OE for 1790 and 1800 from Ira Berlin, *Slaves Without Masters: The Free Negroe in the Antebellum South* (Oxford: Oxford University Press, 1974), pp. 396–97; OE for 1790 from Morgan and Nicholls, op. cit., p. 218.

55. Free black figures and figures for the South are from Berlin, *Slaves Without Masters,* pp. 46, 396–97, except for the Virginia slave population figures, the sources for which are listed in Table I.

56. Kulikoff, "'Prolifick' People," pp. 404–405, 423; Kulikoff, "The Origins of Afro-American Society in Tidewater Maryland and Virginia, 1700 to 1790," *William and Mary Quarterly* (1978): 231, 245; Morgan, "Piedmont Virginia," in Carr, et. al., pp. 438, 441–44.

57. Winley, *Runaway Slave Advertisements;* also Rose, *Documentary History,* p. 56.

58. "Virginia-born" includes mulattoes; "Other-born" includes Caribbean islands, Pennsylvania, Jersey, Rhode Island, and New York.

59. Morgan, "Piedmont Virginia," in Carr, et.al., eds., p. 441.

60. Carter quote is from Terrence W. Epperson, "Race and the Disciplines of the Plantation," *Historical Archaeology* (1990): 29.

61. Anonymous, *A Concise Historical Account of All the British Colonies* (Dublin, 1776), p. 211; John Woolman, *The Journal of John Woolman* (Philadelphia: J Cruckshank, 1774), p. 59; St. George Tucker, quoted in Rose, *Documentary History,* p. 83.

62. Thomas Anbury, *Travels Through the Interior Parts of America,* volume 2 (London, 1789), p. 434; Stampp, *Peculiar Institution,* p. 141.

63. Quoted in Rose, ed., *Documentary History,* p. 52.

64. Thomas Jefferson, *Notes on the State of Virgina,* edited by William Peden (Chapel Hill: University of North Carolina Press, 1954), p. 162.

65. John Davis, *Travels of Four Years and a Half in the United States of America; During 1798, 1799, 1800, 1801, and 1802* (London: R. Edwards, 1803), p. 92.

66. Graham Russell Hodges, ed., *Black Itinerants of the Gospel: The Narratives of John Jea and George White,* edited by Graham Russell Hodges (Madison, Wis.: Madison House, 1993), p. 94.

67. Winley, *Runaway Slave Advertisements,* pp. 25, 47–48, 282, 290, 292, 258, 361.

68. See Winley, *Runaway Slave Advertisements,* passim.

69. Quoted in Davies, *Duty of Christians,* pp. 33–34.

70. Compare Joyce Chaplin, "Slavery and the Principle of Humanity: A Modern Idea in the Early Lower South," *Journal of Social History* (1990): 299–316.

71. Windley, *Runaway Slave Advertisements.* "A." tallies descriptions of "pleasing countenance" and includes the phrases: talks much, talkative, shows teeth, insinuating, brisk, lively, genteel, smiling, good, well, innocent look, cheerful, artful look; "B." is "downcast look" and includes: surly, grim, sour, sly, humble, serious, grave, grum, air of a sailor, modest, sheepish, low, generally hangs his head when spoken to, distressed, sulky, apt to cry, sluggish, sneaking; "C." is "bold/impudent" and includes: roguish, forward, wild look, saucy, smart, arrogant, loud, brazen, proud, knows everything, huffy, walks grand and strong; "D." is "stutters/stammers" and includes: faulters much when speaking, shows whites of eyes much when spoken to.

72. Based on an analysis of the 127 entries in Winley, *Runaway Slave Advertisements,* that include comments about the "character" of the fugitive slave.

73. Richard S. Dunn, "Black Society," in Berlin and Hoffman, eds., *Slavery and Freedom;* Morgan, "Piedmont Virginia"; Morgan and Nicholls, "Slaves in Piedmont Virginia."

74. Figures for 1755, 1782, and 1790 tabulated from the totals and frequencies given in Morgan and Nicholls, "Slaves in Piedmont Virginia," p. 218.

75. Louis B. Wright and Marion Tinling, eds., *Quebec to Carolina in 1785–1786: Being the Travel Diary and Observations of Robert Hunter, Jr., a Young Merchant of London* (San Marino: Huntington Library, 1943), p. 212.

76. Robert Sutcliff, *Travels in Some Parts of North America, in the Years 1804, 1805, & 1806* (London: Longman, Hurst, 1815), pp. 65, 69.

77. Compare with the counties along the littoral tidewater (Northumberland, Lancaster, Middlesex, Gloucester/Matthews, York, Elizabeth City, Norfolk Co., Princess Anne):

LITTORAL TIDEWATER POPULATION

Group	1755	1790	1800	1810	1820
N =	46,426	63,439	58,726	65,144	61,883
Black	23,130	31,792	29,980	34,043	30,793
White	23,296	31,647	28,746	31,101	31,090
% Black	49.8%	50.1%	51%	52%	49.7%

78. Morgan and Nicholls, "Slaves in Piedmont Virginia," p. 238. Cf. with Morgan, "Piedmont Virginia," p. 449; Kulikoff see *Tobacco and Slaves,* p. 330.

79. Based on listings in Augusta Fothergill and John Mark Naugle, comps., *Virginia Tax Payers 1782–87, Other Than Those Published by the United States Census Bureau* (Baltimore: Genealogical Publishing, 1978). I chose the counties of three areas within the Black Belt: the Mattaponi River region (Caroline, King William, and King and Queen); Dinwiddie and Prince George; and Spotsylvania, Louisa, Goochland.

80. Kinlessness ("natal alienation") and generalized dishonor are, according to Orlando Patterson's comparative social theory of slavery, structural elements in the intellectual architecture of any slave system. The assertion of kinfulness and of honorance by descendants of Afri-

cans calls into question some of Patterson's basic assumptions, and suggests that an historically oriented and African-centered rethinking of these issues is in order; see Patterson, *Slavery and Social Death: A Comparative Study* (Cambridge: Harvard University Press, 1982).

81. Compare E. Franklin Frazier's statement: "The enslavement of the Negro not only destroyed the traditional African system of kinship and other forms of organized social life but it made insecure and precarious the most elementary form of social life which tended to sprout anew, so to speak, on American soil—the family" (*Negro Church,* p. 13). Gutman's *Black Family* is an extended refutation of these older assertions.

82. Paulding, *Letters from the South,* pp. 120–21; William N. Blane, *Travels through the United States and Canada* (London: Baldwin, 1828), p. 226.

83. Burwell, *Reminiscences,* p. 4.

84. Rose, ed., *Documentary History,* p. 19.

85. Winley, *Runaway Slave Advertisements,* pp. 299, 180, 262, 263, 389; the others are pp. 111, 125, 144, 187, 254, 169.

86. Compare with the thirty-one percent with imputed motivation to get out of the colony or total escape from Virginia, and the twenty-six percent to pass as free somewhere else.

87. Numbers refer to advertisements rather than to individual slaves. "A." tallies those that mention returning to a relation; "B.," those that mention running away with an accompanying relation; and "Y.," the combination of A. and B.

88. Schoepf, *Travels,* p. 45.

89. Edward L. Ayers, *Vengeance and Justice: Crime and Punishment in the 19th-Century South* (New York: Oxford University Press, 1984), p. 13.

90. Wyatt-Brown, *Southern Honor,* p. 14.

91. See John C. Willis, "Behind 'Their Black Masks': Slave Honor in Antebellum Virginia," M.A. thesis, University of Virginia, 1987; see also Willis, "From the Dictates of Pride to the Paths of Righteousness," pp. 37–55.

92. Willis, "Slave Honor and Christianity," pp. 21–52.

93. See examples in Winley, *Runaway Slave Advertisements,* pp. 33, 39, 149, 159, 248, 284, 345, 329, 362.

94. Ibid., pp. 202, 367, 383. In fact, all runaways could be seen as people who had fled the "field of honor"; see Willis, "'Their Black Masks.'"

95. Kulikoff, *Tobacco and Slaves;* Morgan, "Piedmont Virginia."

96. See, for example, Winley, *Runaway Slave Advertisements,* pp. 130, 139, 142, 190, 219, 341, 94, 284, 300, 255.

97. Anbury, *Travels,* p. 435.

98. Winley, *Runaway Slave Advertisements,* pp. 255, 284, 299–300.

99. Winley, *Runaway Slave Advertisements,* p. 312; see also pp. 107, 108, 120, 316, 246, and passim.

100.   Marquis de Chastellux, *Travels in North America, in the Years 1780, 1781, and 1782,* volume 2 (London: G. G. J. & J. Robinson, 1787), p. 198.

101.   Jefferson, *Notes,* p. 138; also see racist statements on pp. 138–43.

102.   Wright and Tinling, eds., *Quebec to Carolina,* p. 257. He meant that Londoners had no idea of the difficulty of travelling in Virginia.

"This City Has Too Many Slaves Joined Together":

The Abolitionist Crisis in Salvador, Bahia, Brazil, 1848–1856

DALE T. GRADEN

On October 15, 1850, President Francisco Gon-
calves Martins of the Province of Bahia declared that slaves and free
Africans would no longer be allowed to sail in the small boats that plied
the harbor of Salvador. Invoking a law passed more than two years earlier, the president stated that only free Brazilians could transport persons
and goods in the port. In public statements, Martins portrayed his initiative as an enlightened abolitionist act that would create immediate
employment for some five hundred free workers. Concerned about a
violent response by black workers to his decree, Martins requested that
six hundred police be stationed at the docks. On November 1, this transition to free labor occurred without incident. Each year for the following thirty-seven years (until 1887), Bahians celebrated implementation
of the law as a progressive initiative of their political leaders with regards
to slave labor.[1]

Martins's private correspondence reveals this important episode in a
different light. Writing to the imperial minister of state, Martins claimed
that the law insured that Brazilians, not Africans, would be responsible

for servicing the small traffic of the port. Martins emphasized that one of his goals was to improve the economic status of this segment of the urban working class. Martins expressed his desire to provide opportunities for free workers throughout the city, so "that we might be able to free ourselves of the present necessity of having joined together so many slaves in this city."[2] In other words, Martins sought to lessen fears of potential slave violence directed at the white minority (one-third of the population) residing in Salvador.

The comments of President Martins reflect some of the profound social tensions felt by Bahian slave owners in 1850. The second largest slave port in the New World, Salvador or its environs was the destination of some 1.3 million African slaves over the course of more than three centuries.[3] In many ways, Salvador was an African city. Increasingly fearful of this African presence, the Bahian elite faced a mid-century crisis that can be traced to three sources: slave resistance; the outbreak of a yellow fever epidemic; and the appearance of formal abolitionist expression in Salvador. This crisis atmosphere existed for eight years, with varying levels of intensity. Its resolution came about with the end of the international slave trade to Brazil in 1850, sending slaves out of the province as part of an internal slave trade, and as a result of a cholera epidemic in 1855–1856, which devastated the slave population of Salvador and Bahia. After 1856 the institution of slavery remained an integral part of the regional economy until slave resistance and a resurgent abolitionist movement forced an emancipation decree signed by Princess Isabel in 1888.

SALVADOR IN THE FIRST HALF OF THE NINETEENTH CENTURY

As a port city with a large protected harbor, Salvador became one of the largest and wealthiest urban centers in the Americas by the late eighteenth century. The upper part of the city included the homes of the Bahian elite; a lower section near the harbor housed slaves and poor whites. One historian has divided the urban population into four categories. A small elite was composed of planters, merchants, church and state officials, and high-ranking military officials. A second tier might be described as a small upper-middle class, which included professionals, highly-skilled artisans, and persons of some influence in the employ of the church, state, and military. A third rank included persons who sold goods on the streets of the city, soldiers, workers of various sorts, and lower-level professionals. The bottom of this social hierarchy included slaves and a marginalized element who owned few material goods and possessed few skills to offer to a prospective employer.[4]

Salvador and its port are surrounded by a fertile area known as the Reconcavo. Some sixty miles long and up to thirty miles wide, plantations and small farms situated throughout the Reconcavo produced a wide variety of goods for domestic and international markets, including sugarcane, tobacco, cassava, coffee, and a variety of other crops.[5] Slaves, "freedmen" (former slaves) and free persons of color transported these products from hinterland to the port city on small boats, which were then sold in Salvador or loaded on sailing ships. Such contacts helped to create a communication system that spread information rapidly from countryside to city and back again.

To satisfy the demand for plantation and urban labor, Bahian planters and merchants imported thousands of African slaves during the first half of the nineteenth century. The disappearance of agricultural exports from the Caribbean island of Saint Domingue after the Haitian Revolution (1791–1804), combined with steadily increasing sugar production in the Bahian Reconcavo, resulted in a booming international slave trade through the port of Salvador. David Eltis has estimated that sailing vessels transported at least 318,000 slaves to Bahia between 1801 and 1851.[6] These women and men originated from various locations in Africa, including Mozambique, Angola, Cabinda, the Kongo, and the Mina Coast (present-day western Nigeria, the Republic of Benin, Togo, and Ghana).

Bahia became renowned for its rebellious slaves. Between 1807 and 1835, slave owners and provincial authorities confronted more than twenty rural and urban slave revolts. The most famous of these became known as the Revolt of the Malês, an urban rebellion that broke out in Salvador in January, 1835. Led by Muslim Nagô slaves, more than seventy African slaves and freedmen died during the uprising. In the aftermath of the rebellion, some five hundred Africans faced a variety of punishments, including execution and deportation back to Africa or other parts of the empire. The Revolt of the Malês was the largest urban slave revolt in the history of the Americas, and left an enduring legacy of fear among the Brazilian elite. As in the Western world of the late twentieth century, a deep distrust of Arabic language and Islamic religion pervaded Bahian (and Brazilian) society after 1835.[7] Many Bahian merchants and planters linked the Revolt of the Malês with the successful Revolution of Saint Domingue led by African slaves. In a speech in the imperial senate in June, 1843, for example, one influential representative inquired of his compatriots, "are you able to conceive of security in Brazil with this population [of African slaves] . . . are you not able to again see the smoke [from the burned sugar plantations] of the sacrificed victims of Haiti?"[8]

African-Brazilian cultural expression flourished in Salvador in the 1840s. Black men from distinct African ethnic origins joined *cantos* (literally, "corners" of freed and slave workers). The captain of the canto would often speak or chant in his native African dialect when directing his work crew. African cantos transported persons and goods up the windy streets of Salvador from the beaches of the port to the affluent homes of the upper city. Even the most critical European observers noted the physical strength, versatility, and linguistic skills of the cantos. James Wetherell wrote in 1851:

> I have seen immense blocks of wood, with thirty blacks and upwards carrying them, for all the world like an immense centipede. During the time of carrying these heavy burdens through the streets they sing a kind of chorus, a very useful manner of warning persons to get out of the way, as the footfall is not heard in the surrounding bustle. This chorus generally consists of one of the blacks chanting a remark on anything he sees, and the others come in with a chorus of some ridiculous description, which is seldom varied, however much the recitative solo part may. Thus a kind of march, time and time, is kept up.[9]

Candomblé ceremonies (African religious expression) also preserved African culture in Salvador and other cities and towns in the empire. Derived from the Bantu language, the noun *candomblé* is derived from the verb *ku-don-ba* or *kulomba,* meaning to praise, pray, or invoke.[10] Given the large presence of Yoruba Nagô slaves and freemen in Bahia in the first half of the nineteenth century, Nagô traditions had great influence on *candomblé* practices. Other "nations" that had particular influence in Bahian *candomblé* included Jeje and Angola. More specific ethnic classifications that appeared in the *candomblé* rites celebrated by these three "nations" included Kêtu, Alakêto, Efan, Ijexâ, Ebá, Mina Nagô, Tapa, Kongo, and Mina Jeje. Other worshippers of *candomblé* found inspiration from Muslim Malê and *caboclo* (mixture of Amerindian and African) spirits.[11] *Candomblé* most often took place at night in remote locations in the city. Paying homage to the African *orixás* (gods) at houses of *candomblé* encouraged resistance and pride among Africans and African Brazilians. Provincial authorities viewed the practice of *candomblé* with particular suspicion, believing that such worship fomented subversion and potential rebellion. The sounds of late-night drumming that emanates from *terreiros* (sacred grounds of the house) of *candomblé* today in Salvador continues to offend and create unease among many Bahians.

The massive influx of slaves along the coast of Brazil created great anxiety among imperial officials. Brazil received its largest number of slaves ever between 1846 and 1850 (208,900 into Rio de Janeiro and 45,000 into Bahia).[12] Political leaders and citizens lamented that continued importation of African slaves heightened the potential of an upsurge in slave revolts.[13] The Marquês de Abrantes, Miguel Calmon do Pin e Almeida, a *senhor de engenho* (owner of a sugar plantation) from Bahia, succinctly analyzed the situation before his colleagues in the imperial senate. He stated that Brazil had failed to support British efforts to end the traffic in slaves because of a long tradition of Portuguese and Brazilian involvement in slave trading, weak governments and financial instability, a small naval force, and a "spirit of resistance" among the people against any authority.[14] Another *fazendeiro* (owner of a large estate) from Rio de Janeiro, Honório Hermeto Carneiro Leão, contended that

> it is in our interest [to fulfill treaty obligations with the British] because the importation of slaves had become excessive, because the provinces from Bahia southward had become overloaded with slaves; their number was not in proportion with the number of free persons. It was in our interest, in the best interests of our future security, to act, thereby preventing the continuation of slave importations which steadily increased the threat of danger to us.[15]

Similar to the instability witnessed in many urban centers of Europe, events in Salvador and other parts of the empire in the year 1848 and subsequent months should be viewed as part of a critical historical juncture.[16]

1848–1850: THE TERMINATION OF THE INTERNATIONAL SLAVE TRADE TO BRAZIL

Internal pressures within Brazil merit close scrutiny for understanding why Pedro II and imperial ministers supported an end to the international slave trade to Brazil. By early 1848, slave owners in Salvador wondered if the arrival of so many slaves in Bahia and other parts of the empire might not be creating the potential for a major upheaval. An outbreak of a yellow fever epidemic in late 1849 in

Salvador further fueled the debate over the implications of continued high numbers of Africans being brought through the port. These factors, combined with British naval actions on the high sea and along the Brazilian coast, resulted in passage of the Queirós Law of September, 1850, which ended the international slave trade by providing for provisions for enforcement of the legislation.[17]

Concern over a potential slave uprising can be seen in treatment of *libertos* ("freedpersons," or former slaves) by the provincial government. African *libertos* had played an important role in the 1835 Revolt of the Malês. Laws passed soon after that rebellion placed severe restrictions on their personal freedom. One law passed on May 13, 1835, placed a 10,000 reis (about $5 US) tax on all *libertos* residing in the city. City officials requested information about the location of apartments and living arrangements of *libertos*. Out of an urban population of 54,652, *libertos* made up a mere 4.6 percent (approximately 2,508 people, 993 male and 1,515 female). Nevertheless, the belief that this minority presented special problems pervaded official opinion. In 1846 the provincial government exempted an African Nagô freedwoman named Sabina da Cruz from payment of the personal tax. Amazingly, the reason given for this special treatment was she had provided important testimony during the trials of the rebellious Malês eleven years earlier. Two years later, the African freedman Duarte Mendes also learned that he would no longer have to bear the burden of the tax "due to the services he had provided during the insurrection of 1835." Public notices offered a reward of 10,000 reis (about $50 US) to any *libertos* who provided information concerning plans for a "conspiracy or insubordination" involving slaves or *libertos*.[18]

Official correspondence reflects increasing elite fears between 1848 and 1850. The military commander for Bahia complained that he lacked sufficient forces to insure public security in Salvador. "This capital is absolutely without sufficient defenses . . . in case of a slave insurrection, without doubt we will encounter major difficulties because we lack the means to repress an insurrection the instant it appears."[19] Comandante Coelho pointed out that from his earlier experiences with slave revolts in Bahia, soldiers on horseback fought best with lances, swords, and pistols. He considered rifles to be unwieldy and dangerous in that bullets often entered the houses of innocent persons.[20] Other military officials reflected on their experiences fighting in the hilly streets of Salvador and in the forests of the interior of the province. Barão Caxias, Luís Alves de Lima e Silva, criticized lances as ineffective weapons incapable of protecting soldiers from insurgent slaves. He supported the use of rifles and swords.[21] In response to these suggestions, the president of Bahia requested from the Minister of War that the number of calvary troops stationed in Bahia be increased to one hundred men.[22]

Slaves and *libertos* most likely observed closely the words and actions of urban slave owners. Many blacks residing in Salvador had lived through the Revolt of the Malês and remembered this dramatic episode. Although few documents exist that might enable the historian to delve into the thoughts of Bahian slaves, there can be little doubt that the African-Brazilian population of the city hated their masters and would do anything to undermine the slave regime. The recent arrival of thousands of Africans made the moment propitious for organized acts of resistance. Many slaves fled at night to hidden *quilombos* (escaped slave communities) outside the city. Implementation of the 1848 law that forbade slaves and freedmen from laboring in the port occurred due to a perception that blacks had control over a strategic location in the city. Certainly black sailors knew about British attempts to suppress the international slave trade. A municipal decision to modernize the water system of Salvador meant that slaves would no longer be allowed to transport water through the city or have access to private homes.[23] Police searches of the homes of *libertos* and repression of *candomblé* ceremonies further demonstrated the elite's desire to undermine communication networks and the spread of political consciousness.

Within this tense and polarized milieu, a yellow fever epidemic rose its ugly head. In the months following its outbreak in October 1849, the epidemic spread through the city of Salvador and into the interior of the province of Bahia. One historian estimates that within five months, 1,600 persons died in Salvador and another 549 in the Reconcavo.[24] President Martins claimed that 100,000 Bahians had become infected in a short period. He further observed that few slaves and "free Africans" (Africans who had been given freedom by the British after their slave ships had been intercepted on the high sea) had become sick. Martins expressed concern that the epidemic lessened the capacity of police and militia troops to control the slave population of Salvador.[25] The epidemic quickly spread to other parts of the empire. One observer estimated that some 12,000 people died in hospitals and private houses in Rio de Janeiro during the year 1850.[26]

Several Bahian and imperial ministers believed that the yellow fever epidemic could be traced to the international slave trade. Sailors from a ship originating in New Orleans most likely carried the sickness into the port of Salvador. The *Brasil* had visited Cuba on its journey. In Rio de Janeiro, city health officials also pointed to the large number of slaving vessels with holds left filthy from carrying hundreds of Africans for weeks on the high sea as a logical source for the spread of an epidemic. In the imperial Senate, Senhor Alves Branco stated that "everything [that I have seen] leads me to believe that the yellow fever epidemic that has spread so quickly among us can only be understood as originating due to the African slave trade."[27] The epidemic combined with slave resistance made most Brazilians leery of continued importations of Africans.

Until early 1850 British naval actions had failed to stem the importation of African slaves into Bahia and other ports of Brazil. In spite of huge expenditures and the presence of British ships along the African coast, little had been accomplished in terms of effective suppression. One suggestion to force an end of the slave trade came from the pen of James Hudson, the British chargé d'affaires in Brazil. He urged a British naval blockade of Bahia, because slaves in Salvador and the nearby Reconcavo had "attempted on more than one occasion to throw off their yoke and establish themselves in freedom. If that port is blockaded and a position of which I shall speak later near it is occupied, it is almost certain that the negroes will not let such an occasion of securing their freedom escape." Hudson believed that a slave revolt would mean that "the existence of slavery itself in other portions of Brazil would be vitally affected."[28] The British government decided against this tactic. Instead, in early 1850 it intensified naval actions on the high seas and along the Brazilian coast with dogged pursuit of slaving vessels.

An important question regarding the slave trade to Brazil revolves around why it ended in 1850. David Eltis has noted that "the shift [in Brazilian popular opinion] in favor of suppression was profound . . . yet the strength and speed of the change remain something of a puzzle."[29] It would appear that one reason why the British navy acted with unprecedented confidence and determination in 1850 was a perception of increased popular support within Brazil. Eltis observes that "the fact remains that it was the Brazilians and not the British that closed down the slave-importing operations."[30] Support among many Brazilians for an end to the trade can be traced to popular fears of slave resistance, a response to international abolitionist pressures, anti-African biases among all classes of white Brazilians, and working-class hostility toward urban slave workers. In November 1850 Pedro II signed the Queirós law, which brought an end to the slave trade. The mid-century "abolitionist crisis," in the words of Eugene Genovese, was partially resolved by the demise of the international slave trade to Brazil.[31]

"IT IS A CRITICAL EPOCH, AN EPOCH OF RENOVATION": ABOLITIONIST DISCOURSE AT MID-CENTURY

Out of the debates over ending the international slave trade, important discussions evolved over the future of slavery in Brazil. A radical minority surfaced which called for an immediate abolition of the institution of slavery. Powerful planters and merchants rejected such a proposition, claiming that enslaved Africans could not be trusted to act responsibly as free citizens. A myriad of political and economic forces precluded a quick resolution of the slavery question. International abolitionist pressures continued to mount. At the same time, however, an expanding international economy encouraged slave owners to protect their investment in human property. Some of the richest insights into nineteenth-century mentality in Brazil can be found in the spoken and written discourse of the early 1850s.

British abolitionist initiatives had a profound impact upon Brazilian actions and ideas. In 1808, Great Britain had outlawed the slave trade to its possessions and to the United States. In 1834, the British government passed legislation that freed all slaves in its possessions in the British Caribbean. In the 1840s, British pressures to end the international slave trade to Brazil made it increasingly costly to carry on the trade in African slaves. Several influential Brazilians paid homage to such enlightened initiatives. They argued that British commitment reflected Christian thought emanating from the center of a great empire. In the words of Senhor Hollanda Cavalcanti de Albuquerque, "this sentiment [to end the trade in slaves] . . . is not solely [an initiative] of the British government, it is of the British nation, it is the son of erudition emanating from great nations."[32] The Marques de Abrantes claimed that the Europeans acted "out of the profound conviction that the repression [of the slave trade] is absolutely necessary so that Brazil could improve its moral and material status, and arrive at a level of civilization and prosperity to which it has the right to aspire."[33]

Not surprisingly, the decision to end the international slave trade inspired many representatives to offer their opinion about the implications of the Queirós law. Few members of the imperial senate supported immediate emancipation in its wake. Nevertheless, several expressed their views on how to ensure a stable work force in the second half of the century. The Bahian planter Senhor Montezuma pointed to a resurgence in sugar production in the British Caribbean several years after the emancipation decree. He emphasized that less investment in slaves meant more capital available for modernization of agricultural machinery and factories in Brazil.[34] Various senators encouraged immigration of free Africans, Chinese, and light-skinned Europeans as a source of cheap labor in the agricultural sector.[35]

Others discouraged immigration. Instead, they focused on the need to educate lower-class Brazilians to cultivate efficiently private plots and thereby not destroy the environment by slash-and-burn practices.[36] Senhor Rodrigues Torres called for laws to protect individual liberties, improved communication, better education in the arts, and more stable credit institutions to encourage small farmers.[37] In the prophetic words of Senator Paula Souza, "it is unfortunately an epoch of revolution, perhaps an epoch of transformation . . . it is a critical epoch, an epoch of renovation."[38]

In Salvador the appearance of an abolitionist society in 1850 created shock waves throughout the city. The unknown founders of the "Philanthropic Society, established in the capital of Bahia to benefit those Brazilians who had the misfortune to be born slaves" modeled their organization on the example of *cantos* and black brotherhoods that had existed for decades in Salvador. The statutes allowed for the society to be composed of both free persons and twenty-five Brazilian-born slaves. Slaves could only join with permission from their owners. Money paid into an emancipation fund by the slave members would be used to purchase freedom for themselves or other slaves. The Philanthropic Society failed to receive official sanction from the provincial government. Not surprisingly, the chief of police of Salvador prohibited any public meeting of the society.

Two years later students from the Faculty of Medicine founded the "Second of July Emancipation Society." Given the bourgeois background of its members, this organization was viewed with less suspicion and received sanction to meet from the police. Similar to other emancipation societies founded in subsequent years in Salvador, the "Second of July" group tended to be conservative in its outlook. The society did not call for immediate abolition. Lasting for a few years, it dissolved after having accomplished little. The group did use their finances to purchase freedom for a few slaves. Its members included José Luiz de Almeida Couto, Aristides Cezar Spinola Zama, and Jeronymo Sodré Pereira, all of whom made significant contributions to the abolitionist movement in later years.[39]

Journalists condemned slave owners by writing scathing denuncia-tions of government corruption and the immorality of exploiting en-slaved black workers. The masthead of *O Argos Bahiano* of January 30, 1851, included the words *"Está acabado o tempo de enganar os homens"* (The time has ended to delude all men [or the people]). In a front-page ar-ticle, a writer alluded to President of Bahia Francisco Martins as a "pre-varicator" who had become one of the wealthiest men in the province by paying off judges. The author described the various mansions and estates owned by the president. He noted that many slaves had recently been illegally transported to Martins's plantation in the Reconcavo. The article analyzed the way in which Martins had used another newspaper, *Justiça,* to influence public opinion and portray his leadership in a good light. Another article entitled "The Present Crisis" claimed that "the present president of the province . . . has allowed the barbarous slave traders to act with impunity, and from them he hopes for everything, and for them he will sacrifice everything." A third piece included the statement "the Bahian people do not want the traffic [in slaves], they detest it, they find it abominable — because there is plenty of evidence that the traffic, that slavery, is the most powerful element causing the present decadence, and it will bring future ruin to Bahia."[40]

Although only about one-quarter of Salvador's inhabitants could read, critical ideas concerning the international abolitionist movement filtered with ease into Bahia. Radicals and conservatives both read news-paper accounts of recent French and Danish emancipation decrees of 1848 in the Caribbean, and the demands for greater democratic free-doms in the European revolutions of 1848. The appearance of formal abolitionist expression in Salvador in 1850 inspired liberals and enslaved blacks alike.

An important question arises as to why the pressures for emancipa-tion at this juncture had virtually no impact. The time would have seemed to be opportune, given the demise of the slave trade. How did planters and merchants defend themselves from critics who employed enlightenment ideals to legitimize their attacks on slavery? To see how the elite retained its hegemony in the decade of the 1850s goes a long way toward understanding why slavery continued to flourish in Brazil until 1888.

RESOLUTION OF THE ABOLITIONIST CRISIS, 1850–1856

To offset abolitionist criticism, defenders of slav-ery responded on many fronts. They spoke out in public forums, published articles and pamphlets legitimizing their position, maintained strict vigilance over communication networks, and employed police forces and soldiers to repress dissent. This elite had tradition on their side; slavery was a deeply entrenched institution in Brazil that would not easily be destroyed. In Bahia it would once again be an epidemic that brought full resolution to the crisis in that province.

Members of the imperial senate pointed to the positive impact of Brazilian owners on their slaves. Several representatives noted that slaves fared better on plantations in Brazil than they did in the factories of Europe. "Everybody knows that a part of the population of Europe . . . suffers more than do our slaves, because they suffer from hunger, which our slaves do not suffer from."[41] In a speech in the senate, the statements of the Pernambucan senator Hollanda Cavalcanti related the reactionary and paternalistic outlook of the master class:

> A slave in Brazil is happier than a slave in Africa; I am not merely theorizing when I say this; I spent years in Africa . . . I never saw one individual give freedom to a slave . . . Go to the market [in Brazil] to purchase fish, birds, fruits and vegetables, and you will see that the majority of persons selling those goods are negros [sic] who still have the mark of their nation on their faces; . . . Do you want further evidence of how Brazil treats it slaves? Go to the notary's office where personal testaments are deposited, and you will see how much generosity has been extended to them; . . . go to our fazendas, our plantations, and you will find *libertos,* who have received their freedom in return for services offered to their masters; and you don't have to go to the third generation: many slaves who came from Africa have been freed, and if the constitution does not give them Brazilian citizenship, it offers it to their children when they are free. Which nation, in what part of the world, do persons of mixed race have the prerogatives which they have in Brazil? And it is going to be the English who are going to come and teach us philanthropy![42]

In spite of such a biased and incorrect reading of history, such ideas found a large audience. Not only did such an interpretation help to deflect international abolitionist criticism in the short term, but it helped forge an ideology depicting a beneficent white elite in Brazil that lasted well into the twentieth century in the form of the myth of "racial democracy".[43]

Anti-slavery advocates failed to undermine the power of the master class for other reasons. An expanding international capitalist economy meant that slavery remained profitable in Brazil, in Cuba, and in the

United States. Slavery had been a malleable institution since its origins in the New World, and this could be seen with particular clarity in nineteenth-century Brazil. Owners moved their slave property at will, from urban employment to rural, and from one part of the nation to another. Popular prejudice among free Brazilians against blacks and mulattoes precluded a quick transition to a free labor system. Perhaps most importantly, the imperial government created no viable immigration program (as would occur in the 1880s) to provide cheap labor to planters.

In Salvador, as in other cities along the coast, merchants and planters pointed to the recent history of the United States to defend a pro-slavery stance. The international slave trade to the United States had ended in 1808. In the following decades, the slave system in the American South had expanded both geographically (cotton into the deep South) and in terms of numbers of slaves (four million by 1860). The American South was the only plantation region in the Americas where the slave population increased.

Brazilian planters hoped to emulate the example of the United States.[44] Such a strategy can be seen from the registries of ships that transported slaves out of Bahia to Rio de Janeiro as part of the internal slave trade to southern regions of the empire after 1850. Vessels that one would have expected to carry a majority of males to labor in expanding coffee plantations instead included high percentages of women. This most likely occurred not only because southern planters appreciated the abilities of female workers, but also for reasons of potential fertility. For example, the brigantine *Patacho,* which traveled from Bahia to Rio de Janeiro in August 1851, included twenty-four females out of the total of forty-seven slaves on board.[45]

Wealthy inhabitants of Salvador concerned about social tensions in their province sent many slaves south as part of the internal trade. Precious documents from Bahia demonstrate that "free Africans" of Nagô origin — African slaves who had been taken from intercepted slaving vessels by the British — created a public furor in Salvador due to their rebellious behavior. Government officials decided it best to send many of these Africans into the south, and hoped that "free Africans" of different ethnic origins — blacks who would not create disturbances — might be imported back into Bahia. The large numbers of slaves sent out of Bahia to Rio de Janeiro and Minas Gerais as part of the internal slave trade led one Bahian in the Chamber of Deputies to request a halt to such exports by 1854. The representative compared the brutalities associated with the internal trade to the recently ended international trade. He believed that the high outflow of slaves would weaken the political influence of the planters and threaten the viability of the slave system.[46]

The urban elite of Salvador responded to the turbulence they observed in their city by carrying out policies of fierce repression against slaves, *libertos,* and whites. Police searched the houses of *libertos,* looking for papers written in Arabic or materials used in Islamic religious ceremonies. Arrests of *libertos* based on flimsy evidence became common. Soldiers enforced strict controls over movement of slaves and *libertos* in the streets of the city and to the countryside. Owners had to pay high fines to extricate slaves from jail who had been caught out on the streets after the ringing of the evening bell. Police invaded houses of *candomblé* and arrested participants. They accused blacks of subversion and immoral acts, along with sheltering fugitive slaves. To the dismay of the provincial government, on several instances police encountered whites partaking of these African celebrations. Although such groups as the "Second of July Emancipation Society" received official permission to gather, it was clearly understood that their proclamations and initiatives could not be inflammatory. At no time during these years did the elite of Salvador consider abolition a possible solution to their problems. Instead, it would appear that the resulting social tensions only increased their racism and determination to control the world around them.

One remarkable incident on the African coast further contributed to a hardening of outlook among Bahian slave owners. The North American brig *Mary Adeline* departed from Rio de Janeiro in April, 1852, destined for the coast of Angola. After being visited by the British steamship *Fire Fly* for evidence of slave trading in early June, the *Mary Adeline* ran aground on a sand bar at Shark's Point near the mouth of the Congo River. Within a day an estimated fifteen hundred to three thousand Africans attacked the boat. They possessed muskets, spears, oars, and cutlasses, along with hooks and poles to climb the side of the ship. The small crew of the *Mary Adeline* fought back by shooting a six-pound cannon that killed several of the Africans. Only with the help of the British ships *Fire Fly* and the *Dolphin* did the *Mary Adeline* manage to get free from the beach and anchor in deep water.

The *Mary Adeline* departed from the Congo River on June 29 and sailed for Bahia. Soon after his arrival in Salvador, Captain A. Oaksmith of the *Mary Adeline* provided a deposition to the United States consul stationed in Bahia. He proudly proclaimed that no Americans had been seriously hurt in the fighting, and that several Africans had died. He thanked the British captains and crews for helping to save the North American ship and its crew. His words are worth noting: "In order that you [John Gillmer, U.S. consul] may be convinced that nothing discreditable was entertained in relation to myself or my flag in connection with the affair [slave trading], I have the honor to transmit to you the accompanying letter from the commander and officers of the 'Dolphin'." In this second note, Lieutenant W. Wood praised the courage of Oaksmith and most of his crew for defending themselves against the "murderous attack of at least 3,000 natives who had assembled for the purpose of plundering valuable cargo."[47]

Many questions are raised by the episode. Did the captain of the *Fire Fly* not find any evidence of slave trading when he boarded the *Mary Adeline* near Loango before the latter ran aground? Why did the *Mary Adeline* attempt to enter the Congo River? It would appear that the North American ship hoped to pick up a cargo of slaves. Why did British ships, one of which was patrolling the coast, come to the aid of the *Mary Adeline?* Most importantly, did the Africans who attacked the ship merely seek its cargo, or was this an act of war against a slaving vessel by Africans who understood that the slave trade to Brazil had been declared an act of piracy two years earlier? The perception that blacks had come close to taking over a ship on the African coast surely convinced many Bahians that a resumption of the slave trade would be unlikely. Furthermore, such resistance in West Africa made abolitionist expression in Brazil even more of a threat to elite interests.

A decrease of many of the social tensions in Salvador inspired by slave resistance and abolitionist dissent related to the cholera epidemic of 1855–1856 (which also included a resurgence of yellow fever). Believed to have arrived in Bahia on the ship *Imperatriz* from Pará, the epidemic spread quickly after July, 1855. During the next ten months, some 9,332 inhabitants of Salvador perished, representing 16.8 percent of the city's population of 56,000.[48] Other regions in the Reconcavo suffered huge population losses as well, including the Cachoeira, Santo Amaro, and Nazaré. One historian estimates as many as 40,000 Bahians died during this devastating epidemic.[49] Hundreds of citizens of Salvador died on roads leading out of the city when they attempted to flee from the dreaded infection. Hundreds more died who had fled from their homes in the Reconcavo seeking what they thought would be respite in Salvador.

The slave and mulatto population of Salvador and the Reconcavo suffered the most from the epidemic. Many urban slaves and free blacks lived in squalid conditions in *favelas* (shacks constructed close to one another, often on the sides of hills), which existed throughout the city. Government officials forced slaves to take the deceased out of private homes and transport them to cemeteries for burial, resulting in infection and death. In the Reconcavo, slaves working on plantations often consumed food of minimal nutritional value and therefore had few natural defenses to fight off the cholera. The epidemic wrought such havoc that elite fears about the large presence of slaves or their capacity to organize an urban revolt diminished significantly. Instead, their concern shifted to consideration of how best to preserve the remaining slave population; how to attract European or Chinese immigrants; and what could be done to expand sugar production, which had declined significantly during the months of the epidemic. The European observer Robert Avé-Lallemant wrote of these years that

> the splendid progress in the production of beat sugar in Europe, on the one hand, and the repression of the slave trade from Africa to Brazil, on the other, came together with an avenging Nemesis, the cholera epidemic, causing the greatest devastation among the slaves of the plantations, thereby having major repercussions in the production of sugar in Bahia, and in general, in the export of that product, not only reducing it in volume, but also reducing its value.[50]

The success of radical social movements is often determined by the size and/or commitment of its following. The number of Africans arriving in Salvador and nearby estates along the coast reached unprecedented levels by 1848 and 1849. New Africans who remained in Salvador surely learned quickly of past revolutionary outbreaks led by slaves. Concerned government officials sought to inhibit slave resistance at mid-century by increasing the size of the police force and by sending slaves out of Salvador into the interior of the province or destinations in the south of the empire. The outbreak of a yellow fever epidemic in 1849–1850 that affected whites far more than blacks added to the reigning social tensions. Abolitionist expression, both international and domestic, forced Bahia's (and Brazil's) elite to defend their position as never before. Bahian slaveholders survived this "critical epoch," an "unfortunate epoch of revolution," by means of violent repression of dissent and due to the ravages of infectious diseases.

NOTES

1. Luís Anselmo da Fonseca, *A escravidão, o clero e o abolicionismo* (Recife: Editora Massangana, 1988), pp. 185–95.
2. President Francisco Goncalves Martins to Secretary of State Visconde de Mont'Alegro, Salvador, Nov. 22, 1850, Arquivo Nacional in Rio de Janeiro, Secção de Poderes Executivos (hereafter cited as ANRJ/SPE), IJJ 9 339.
3. Luís Vianna Filho, *O negro na Bahia*, third edition (Rio de Janeiro: Editora Nova Fronteira, 1988), p. 160. Vianna Filho estimates that 1.3 million African slaves were transported to Brazil, with Rio de Janeiro receiving 38 percent and Bahia 25 percent of the total. This estimate contradicts Joseph Murphy's claim that Salvador was "the largest slave port in the Americas," an interpretation which he incorrectly bases on estimates provided by Philip Curtin; see Murphy, *Working the Spirit: Ceremonies of the African Diaspora* (Boston: Beacon Press, 1994), pp. 45, 211–12.
4. Katia M. de Queirós Mattoso, *Bahia, século XIX: uma província no império* (Rio de Janeiro: Editora Nova Fronteira, 1992), pp. 596–99.
5. B. J. Barickman, "'A Bit of Land, Which They Call Roça': Slave Provision Grounds in the Bahian Recôncavo, 1780–1860," *Hispanic American Historical Review*, 74 (Nov., 1994): 653–66.
6. David Eltis, *Economic Growth and the Ending of the Transatlantic Slave Trade* (New York: Oxford University Press, 1987), pp. 243–44.
7. James Wetherell, *Brazil: Stray Notes from Bahia* (Liverpool: Birkenhead, 1860), p. 138; Chief of Police J. M. Wanderley to police delegate in Cachoeira, Salvador, Mar. 24, 1849, Arquivo Público do Estado da Bahia/Correspondência do chefe da Polícia (hereafter cited as APEB/Polícia), maço 5870, p. 174; Subdelegate of police Manoel Francisco Borges Leitao to chief of police of Salvador, Salvador, Apr. 4, 1853, Arquivo Público do Estado da Bahia/Secção do Arquivo Colonial e Provincial (hereafter cited APEB/SACP), maço 6230.
8. "Sessão em 10 de Junho de 1843", *Anais do senado do império do Brasil* (Rio de Janeiro: Senado Federal, 1978; hereafter cited as *ASIB*), p. 105.
9. Wetherell, *Brazil: Stray Notes*, p. 53; J. da Silva Campos, "Ligeiras notas sobre a vida intima, costumes e religião dos Africanos na Bahia," *Annaes do Arquivo Público da Bahia*, 29 (1943): 291–94.
10. Zeca Ligièro, "Candomblé is Religion-life-art," in *Divine Inspiration: From Benin to Bahia*, edited by Phyllis Galembo (Albuquerque: University of New Mexico Press, 1993), p. 102.
11. Murphy, *Working the Spirit*, pp. 44–49.
12. Eltis, *Economic Growth*, p. 244.
13. "Sessão em 22 de Janeiro de 1850," *ASIB*, pp. 93–94; "Sessão em 27 de

Maio de 1851," *ASIB*, p. 387; "Sessão em 28 de Maio de 1856," *ASIB*, p. 233.

14. "Sessão em 28 de Maio de 1856," *ASIB*, p. 233.

15. "Sessão em 27 de Maio de 1851," *ASIB*, pp. 387–88.

16. Jonathan Sperber, *The European Revolutions, 1848–1851* (Cambridge: Cambridge University Press, 1994).

17. Dale T. Graden, "'A Measure . . . Even of Public Security': Slave Resistance, Social Tensions and the End of the International Slave Trade to Brazil, 1835–1856," *Hispanic American Historical Review* (forthcoming).

18. Anna Amélia Vieira Nascimento, *Dez freguesias da cidade do Salvador: aspectos sociais e urbanos do século xix* (Salvador: Fundação Cultural do Estado da Bahia, 1986), pp. 98–99.

19. Comandante das Armas José Joaquim Coelho to President João Duarte Lisboa Serra, Salvador, Oct. 4, 1848, ANRJ/SPE, IG 1 119.

20. Comandante Coelho to President Francisco Martins, Salvador, Oct. 23, 1848, ANRJ/SPE, IG 1 119.

21. Conde de Caxias to Minister of War Manoel Felezardo de Souza e Mello, Rio de Janeiro, Nov. 3, 1848, ANRJ/SPE, IG 1 119.

22. President Francisco Martins to Minister of War Manoel Felezardo de Souza e Mello, Salvador, Oct. 24, 1848, ANRJ/SPE, IG 1 199.

23. Arnold Wildberger, *Os presidentes da província da Bahia* (Salvador: Typographia Beneditina, 1949), p. 321.

24. Nascimento, *Dez freguesias,* p. 166.

25. President Martins to Minister of the Empire Monte Alegre, Salvador, Jan. 1, 1850, ANRJ/SPE, IJJ 9 339.

26. Sidney Chalhoub, "The Politics of Disease Control: Yellow Fever and Race in Nineteenth Century Rio de Janeiro," *Journal of Latin American Studies,* 25 (Oct., 1993): 441–42.

27. "Sessão em 9 de Setembro de 1850," *ASIB*, p. 519. See also "Sessão em 13 de Maio de 1850," *ASIB*, pp. 16–17.

28. Cited in Eltis, *Economic Growth,* p. 114.

29. Eltis, *Economic Growth,* p. 216.

30. Ibid., p. 214.

31. Eugene D. Genovese, *From Rebellion to Revolution: Afro-American Slave Revolts in the Making of the Modern World* (Baton Rouge: Louisiana State University Press, 1979), p. 111.

32. "Sessão em 27 de Maio de 1850," *ASIB*, p. 127.

33. "Sessão em 28 de Maio de 1856," *ASIB*, p. 234.

34. "Sessão em 24 de Maio de 1851," *ASIB*, pp. 310–11.

35. "Sessão em 6 de Setembro de 1848", *ASIB*, p. 69; "Sessão em 21 de Agosto de 1848", *ASIB*, p. 398.

36. "Sessão em 28 de Maio de 1856," *ASIB*, p. 243.

37. "Sessão em 22 de Janeiro de 1850," *ASIB*, p. 101.

38. "Sessão em 27 de Maio de 1850," *ASIB*, p. 106.

39. Fonseca, *A escravidão*, p. 244.

40. *O Argos Bahiano* (Salvador), Jan. 30, 1851, pp. 1–3.

41. "Sessão em 27 de Maio de 1850," *ASIB*, p. 110.

42. Ibid., p. 130.

43. Carl N. Degler, *Neither Black nor White: Slavery and Race Relations in Brazil and the United States* (Madison: University of Wisconsin Press, 1986), pp. 281–92; Michael George Hanchard, *Orpheus and Power: The Movimento Negro of Rio de Janeiro and São Paulo, 1945–1988* (Princeton: Princeton University Press, 1994), pp. 43–74.

44. "Sessão em 28 de Maio de 1851," *ASIB*, p. 404.

45. "Relação do escravos entrados neste porto no dia 3 de Agosto 1851 no Patacho 'Continente' procedente da Bahia,' Rio de Janeiro, Sept. 2, 1851, ANRJ/SPE, IJ 1 710.

46. Robert Edgar Conrad, *World of Sorrow: The African Slave Trade to Brazil* (Baton Rouge: Louisiana State University Press, 1986), pp. 173–74.

47. A. Oaksmith to John S. Gillmer, Salvador, July 26, 1852; and W. Wood to A. Oaksmith, Congo River, June 24, 1852, United States National Archives, Diplomatic Despatches, Brazil, T 331: 1.

48. Nascimento, *Dez freguesias*, p. 161.

49. Johildo Lopes de Athayde, *Salvador e a grande epidemia de 1855* (Salvador: Centor de Estudos Baianos da Universidade Federal da Bahia, 1985), p. 22.

50. Robert Avé-Lallemant, *Viagem pelo norte do Brasil no ano de 1859*, volume 1 (Rio de Janeiro: Instituto Nacional do Livro, 1961), pp. 24–27; cited in Athalyde, *Salvador e a grande epidemia*, pp. 27–28.